A TEXTBOOK FOR LIFE, LOVE AND OUR HUMAN EXISTENCE

WHY OUR WORLD

by TUH

Published by
Top Monkey
3920 Prospect Ave., Suite A
Yorba Linda, CA. 92886
www.TopMonkey.com

All rights reserved. No part of this book may be reproduced or utilized in any form or by any information storage and retrieval system, without advance permission in writing.

Copyright © 2013 Registered by Maria A. Pallante

Office in accordance with title 17 United States Code attests that registration has been made for the work identified as "*Why Our World*". This information has been made part of the Copyright Office records.

Effective Registration Date: December 12 2012

Registration Number: TX 7-614-546

Text, illustrations and compilation.

The movie script "*Great Pyramids of Giza*" encompasses the new-era ideas of "*Why Our World*" while engaging an action-packed storyline. For inquires about this book or movie script please contact Top Monkey.

www.WhyOurWorld.com

ISBN: 0988826607
ISBN-13: 9780988826601
Library of Congress Control Number: 2012924246
CreateSpace Independent Publishing Platform,
North Charleston, SC

TABLE OF CONTENTS

Introduction

Chapter 1 .... Children

Chapter 2 .... Love

Chapter 3 .... The Evils

Chapter 4 .... Positive, Negative, and Balance

Chapter 5 .... The Unconscious Mind

Chapter 6 .... Universe, Time, and Energy

Chapter 7 .... Death and Rebirth

Chapter 8 .... The Ancient Egyptians

Chapter 9 .... Religion

Chapter 10 .... Versions of You

INTRODUCTION

No matter who you are, what your education level is, or how much money you make, you have questions. Many occurrences we live with everyday are puzzling, while others are simple to understand. Some people are ready to accept the information this book will convey; others will choose not to. Regardless of your beliefs or your ability to understand human events that occur in our world, you will be compelled to ponder the information presented by the journey you are about to embark upon.

Current-day educational courses offer little to inform people on the key ingredients required for true happiness and love throughout a lifetime. When people conclude their academic training they are cast carelessly into the world with insufficient practical education. This lack of training results in a failure to achieve basic human goals.

There are conjunctive rules that need to be followed when exploring subjects with many unknown possibilities. To start with, everything is a circle, even if the connection is not visible. There are exceptions to almost every rule. Every action has an equal and opposite reaction. Almost nothing is what it seems. To get a rough estimate of an answer take each variable to its extreme. Finally, completely read a subject before forming an opinion. Basic theories indeed, most of life's mysteries are simple; they just seem complicated because the answer is unknown.

For every action there is an equal and opposite reaction. A profound notion indeed, Newton envisioned this theory not knowing how many applications it would encompass. Everything has a reaction to an action, whether seen or not.

Humans

Humans have existed on this earth about 250,000 years, but how did we arrive or evolve? Some say we have simply evolved from a primate, while others believe a miracle from a god is responsible. A simple evolution from primates seems remote because humans are about one hundred times more complex both emotionally and intellectually, a completely different species.

Additionally, this single chromosome modification that created our human populous was adjusted to produce multiple races of humans. As the primary human

Introduction

evolution cycle began to mature, the residual primate tendencies were bred out, exposing the human form. Ultimately, humans created groups, and eventually small societies were developed.

In most cases, normal evolutionary guidelines that dictate the evolution of a species are followed by extinction of the underdeveloped specimens. This has not occurred for primates. Additionally, why is the "human" style of evolution exclusive to primates and not other animals?

The span of the human race, beginning to end, is much like any life cycle. As a race, humans achieve greatness at the "apex" of our earthly existence.

Currently society has preserved about five thousand years of history. From the years preceding these recordings only bits and pieces can be obtained. Research has produced speculation on ancient civilization living conditions, cultivation and building techniques. These scattered facts have been interpreted many different ways. Unfortunately, most of this information fails to identify traditions, intelligence levels, or purpose correctly.

Life Energy

There are many examples of humans' emotional energy that most people underestimate. Some are subtle, such as a smile, and some are more intense, like jealousy or rage. When a person becomes angry, his heartbeat and adrenaline levels rise, which causes his voice to get louder and face to become flush. Once the event has concluded, the person's energy level is diminished. A rejuvenation period is then required before ambient levels can resume.

This energy transference condition is present in all physical and mental extremities. All emotions convert to a specific type of energy, which then affects a person's life energy. Collectively, these emotions translate into a lifestyle.

Love and hate are emotions that reside at the opposite ends of the energy spectrum. Even though these energies are completely opposite, they can alternate rapidly. When love is removed from a person's life, discomfort is experienced, which is the result of a positive energy being eliminated. When hate is abolished, negative energy is removed, creating a simultaneous energy boost.

Unsurpassed in result, love and hate possess the ability to alter life paths of every person connected though a relationship. The decision to love or hate is rendered based on perspective. A successful life practice includes the ability to acknowledge positive life attributes while ignoring the negative. Acting in a negative manner

Introduction

promotes the attraction of similar energies. The opposite is true for positive actions.

As most people attempt to recall their first memories of life they are successful only back to her fifth birthday. Throughout the birth and infant stages, a person's brain is still developing and is unable to retain early awareness. Let's go one step further back—where is the person's life energy before it originated in the birth process?

When a person is born, a life energy is initiated through the miracle of birth. This life energy is the essence in which the soul is held. Throughout a lifetime, life energy either ascends or descends, depending on the actions and thoughts of the individual. When people die their life energy is transferred out of their body. As this energy passes from lifetime to lifetime, natural likes and dislikes, talents, and shortcomings pursue them. There are virtually endless accounts of highly advanced, knowledgeable, and talented children who inherit skills that far outreach normality.

Human life energy and electrical energy exhibit many of the same characteristics. Electricity works on two basic principles, positive and negative energy. Magnetic energy fields are created from an electronic standpoint. This energy presents itself in organisms as minuscule as bacteria, and as ample as the universe.

Why Our World

The matter from which everything is created was designed to change with time. Therefore, anything in our universe must adhere to this basic principle. Everything in existence is energy, some kind of element in basic form.

Life energy parallels the characteristics of electricity (matter). Like electricity, life energy is controllable and with this control comes possibilities.

Ancient Stories

Most people find comfort in current religious establishments. This pacification is based on a story documented in the past that has endured many generations. While religion supplies many useful attributes, discrepancies among religious establishments have created controversy.

Absent of unequivocal proof, a single religion cannot be awarded superiority while condemning the remaining contenders. Due to the ambiguous nature of the religion inspired stories, some people experience difficulty committing. By design, humans possess the aspiration to improve mental well-being, which drives the need to believe in something more substantial than our current existence.

Introduction

The ancient Egyptians are one of the most controversial and misunderstood societies on earth. Many buildings and statues located on the Giza Plains in Egypt were created in the time period of ancient kings and pharaohs. Among these structural wonders stand four monolithic pyramids and a lion-human hybrid called a "sphinx". Currently, thousands of people visit Egypt every year to see the mystery of these extraordinary human achievements. Many questions still surround these buildings as to their method of construction and purpose. Historians have suggested that these structures were assembled using slaves ruled by force and execution. Others claim the Egyptians used alien assistance.

Throughout our modern-day society, we trust assumptions made about historical events as interpreted by field professionals. But, as we know, professionals can be mistaken (we're only human). These professionals have almost completely translated the ancient Egyptian hieroglyphics, artifacts, and remaining monuments. After years of exploration and countless hours of deliberation, many questions still remain.

It will be the past that teaches us about our future. The ancient Egyptian society represents the "middle of time" for the existence of humans on earth. The Egyptians established one of the first advanced societies on earth and are the actual reason we exist today. Humans have a cycle; each planet in the solar system has a cycle. As one dies, it gives way to a new one. To help understand the basis for the ancient Egyptian goal, we must travel back in time, before the first humans on earth.

Universe

Global space programs have spent years and an astronomical amount of money attempting to unlock the secrets of the universe. While many attempts have been successful in localized space travel, voyages to the outer reaches of the galaxy remain insurmountable. A fuel source capable of interstellar rejuvenation and life-sustaining requirements remain the main obstacles. If these barriers were eventually overcome, a final conundrum presents itself: destination.

As life-producing planets evolve elsewhere in the universe, a comparable situation could transpire similar to the eco system on earth. The phenomenon of life exists on our planet; it would be naïve to believe this condition is exclusive.

The Obvious

Why don't people learn what's right in front of them? It's because they are not ready to understand it. People will learn only what they are ready to learn. As a

Introduction

philosopher once said, "There is no short cut to the path; there is only the path." While our society matures, a new mindset is emerging, no longer are people satisfied with the status quo. We desire a more direct approach, proof if you will, or at least a more believable possibility.

The unknown can drive a person insane. Is there an answer for every question? That's difficult to say, but a problem that can be solved, will be, in time. Things that seemed impossible will become commonplace, our normal evolutionary process. Our earth provides basic rules that every living species must adhere to such as oxygen, water, nourishment, and reproductive cycles. Human life is vastly different than every other life form on earth and is the only form of life that has experienced advanced intelligence evolutions.

If a person observed a civilization of hamsters attempting to build a bicycle instead of a survival system they would assume the hamsters possess a minimal amount of intelligence.

- Enhancing intelligence requires people to assume they know less than the person trying to educate them.
- Intelligence can be gauged only by someone smarter than the person being evaluated.
- Intelligence cannot be judged by a volume of memorized information.

- Intelligence can be judged only by expanding common knowledge.

If our current civilization were headed in the complete wrong direction, would we be able to recognize it? Our present day society may not be composed of the most intelligent people who have existed on this planet. We might just be the current inhabitants living here.

Human existence and purpose on this earth remain a mystery. To solve this mystery, a person must be open to new ideas and explore possibilities outside conventional thinking.

As the world's population grows closer together with more human races becoming commingled, information is needed to stimulate our understanding. This growth will come in the form of answers to our existence.

The ancient Egyptians were the conclusion of the first human (positive) evolution cycle. Their existence provides the information needed to change our world.

Chapter 1
CHILDREN

As infants develop into children their accomplishments are endless. Most kids gain confidence and see the "good" in everyday occurrences. This innocence is the "magic" of life that contributes to the rate of their advancement. In the process of growing into an adolescent, many of these positive attributes are stripped away when the child is prepared for adulthood. Sustaining this previous happiness is sometimes difficult to achieve in the mature phases of life. Is this removal of childhood happiness a normal side effect of adulthood?

Parents

Each parent assumes an individual role in raising a child. These roles are non-gender specific. Young children have a natural proclivity to cling to a sympathetic parent while avoiding the more abrupt parent. Whenever children are frightened, the affectionate parent is the one they flee to, a maternal instinct instilled at birth.

Why Our World

Children can get frustrated in situations they don't understand. This frustration dissipates as the lesson is learned while boosting self-confidence. If a child fails to recognize the answer to a problem, the information is stored in his memory and is available when the problem resurfaces. Information absorption rates vary according to maturity levels.

There are many primary lessons necessary for a child's successful development. These lessons include the importance of other people's feelings and a job well done. An inexperienced child may alienate themselves from peers due to inappropriate behavior. This condition can be alleviated by observation and explanation from a parent. Once the problem has been identified learning can begin. This practice is especially important for sibling relationships.

Parents' influence over their children is unique. Throughout the development stages, particular situations transpire that lend themselves to an accelerated learning experience. These occurrences include such things as the first time a child dresses them self. Once children drop a soiled article of clothing on the floor, instruct them instead to place it into the hamper. This "first time" condition embeds a normal action. These instances occur many times throughout the adolescent stages. Examples include organizing school subjects, allocating homework time, and doing chores. Parents are responsible for

Chapter 1 - Children

instructing their children how to think and feel in these particular situations. This behavioral education is instrumental in developing organizational skills.

Many stages of child rearing are very rewarding for parents, while other aspects are less desirable, such as controlling anger. When raising a child, mishaps are inevitable. These unintentional accidents are the result of a normal education process that is out of the child's control.

The fear aspect of anger is a typical parent-reaction phenomenon that occurs when a child is in immediate danger of injuring themselves or someone else. In this instance, the anger emotion is necessary (within reason) while displaying concern that could possibly thwart a potentially dangerous situation. Directly following this event, communication between the parent and child must transpire to explain the danger while conveying concern and love. This will defuse any negative feelings between the child and parent.

Parental anger is most effective in small doses and should be used (within reason) when extreme conditions exist. Excessive anger from a parent throughout a childhood creates apprehension while damaging the child's self-esteem. Once this relationship is damaged, children lose their "safe zone" and will experience fear, perhaps for the first time.

When accidents occur a parent should happily assist the child to repair or clean up whatever disorder that has transpired. The child learns that no matter what happens in life, it can be fixed, most of the time. This will give the child confidence to try something new, spontaneously and without guidance.

Negative situations are a necessary factor of life that can be an opportunity for a parent and child to grow. Many personality deficiencies in children are caused by parents who fail to recognize their own shortcomings.

When it comes to determining actions for a child of a medical or academic nature, parents have a natural intuition. Once information is compiled from field professionals, the parents (alone) should make their own decision.

It can be advantageous for a parent to reward the child when warranted with material items. This practice should be used with caution to avoid an emotional downfall when these material pacifications fail to continue.

Poor academic performance can create parental disappointment toward a child. This form of anger is based on the parents having a fear of the child possibly becoming a burden on society while jeopardizing the child's happiness and their own. This anger is used as a tool to

Chapter 1 - Children

shock the child into performing better, which is sometimes unsuccessful. Alternatively, this emotional jolt forces children to become unresponsive as they construct a mental defense mechanism designed to help reverse negative feelings created by the attacks.

For a child, parents are like a pair of helping hands located below them (just out of sight), observing their baby bird learning to fly. These helping hands assist only when needed, representing unconditionally love.

Teenagers

As the childhood phase of life comes to a close, a sometimes difficult transition occurs. A once-sweet child can morph into an unruly teenager practically overnight. A parent will start to hear things like, "Going over to my friends to hang out" instead of "Mommy, can I go over to my friend's house and play?" As the process continues, parents become familiar with the terms "Later" and "See ya" followed by the door closing.

When children approach the teenage stage of life, a new-found energy is discovered. This energy is the result of a "freedom" factor produced by the onset of adulthood. This energy causes teens to stay awake longer and sleep in later than they did previously. Teenagers also seem to run forever without the sleep they needed throughout their childhood. This is because the teen is using accumulated "sleep credits" while childhood sleep time restrictions were in place. Teenagers spend these credits, which can last weeks, or even months.

Unfortunately, a certain amount of sleep is instrumental for the ability to make correct decisions and maintain normal behavior. Once a significant amount of sleep credits have been consumed, the teen will start to become unpleasant and experience unusual behavioral outbursts. In severe situations, the teen can experience mood swings that include depression and rage. Once sleep credits have returned to a "normal" level, typical personality characteristics return. If recharging these sleep credits is artificially shorted, it causes exhaustion and a longer rejuvenation period.

Performing crazy antics is a natural occurrence of the teenager experience. These shenanigans are the result of new-found freedom combined with limited inhibitions. Many of these zany acts are nothing more than experiments to experience the reaction of a particular event. Young teenagers experiment in their own direction while looking back for their parents' approval. If parental response is not provided, they feel abandoned and look toward peers for endorsement.

Constricting rules set up by society can slowly erode the energy of most teenagers, who are often forced into

Chapter 1 - Children

conformity by assuming jobs that fail to recognize their individual talent. This failure cause's frustration which may jeopardize the teenagers' self image. Some teenagers respond poorly to authority. Many of these teen tendencies are inherited, while other behavioral traits can be attributed to overbearing parents who produce tension whenever authority is presented.

Aggressive children can impose their physical superiority to humiliate an underdeveloped child. This primal survival instinct provides instant gratification. Teenagers who are consistently degraded abandon their self-worth and allow anyone to control them.

Maturity levels in an experienced teenager are much higher than one of less aptitude. Throughout the teenage years, differences in individual maturity levels can vary greatly and change rapidly. Differences in viewpoints naturally segregate groups into similar types. These communal levels are responsible for the social and academic advancement that set the stage for adulthood.

Most teenagers have a propensity to favor either street or academic intelligence. While the academic option is a structured learning curriculum, the street version is a random situation education that allows teenagers to make their own decisions. Most receive a mixture of both types of education. In some cases, a teenager is subject to extreme conditions of a street or academic education that upsets a balance, which produces frustration and slows development. Acquiring knowledge from both sides of the spectrum produces a well-balanced individual.

Academically, some teenagers deem schoolwork as mundane. These students require a more engaging subject matter that presents a challenge. At the other end of the spectrum is the hopeless underachiever. These students have a hard time fitting in socially while failing academically. These conditions generate frustration that make a teenager feel disconnected, which promotes isolation.

Teenage passion and obsession are both a gift and a curse. When a particular obsession is pacified, the teen can grow and evolve. While the interest boost of an obsession increases production, it can cause an emotional stall as well. This stall can be caused by an excessive duration period while attempting the completion of a goal. If this fixation is unattainable after sufficient effort has been given, it can leave a teenager with a sense of uncertainty. Obsessions hold the key to each step into adulthood.

Parents of a Teenager

From a parent's point of view, it might be uncomfortable to watch as painful physical and mental

Chapter 1 - Children

transformations in their teens occur on the road to becoming a young adult. The parents are now observing their child in a world that offers them a chance to live as "themselves", instead of the person they perceived them to be.

These developmental processes will produce unexpected relationship changes as parents are relieved from the control of their child's life. This alteration can cause a backlash effect that may cause parents to try to control the situation by exerting authority, which means very little to the newly liberated teen.

Successful intervention requires intuition and the ability to navigate situations without creating aggravation. This balance is dependent on the ability to allow a teen to learn a "self- taught" lesson, and knowing when to interject.

Most teenagers are subject to a peaking order that is controlled by one or more dominate members of their group. When supplying information to answer a teenager's question, consider beyond the normal scope of the situation (friendships) to avoid unwanted relationship turmoil.

Use care when informing teenagers of what they are doing wrong. In most cases they already know. Excessive micro-managing from a parent can cause a teenager to pull away, while damaging the relationship. Most serious relationship damage occurs in the teenage years.

If parental interjection occurs only when a negative action is performed, the teen believes mistakes are the only action a parent notices. When teenagers make their own choices, even if they are wrong, an affirmative spin by the parents is beneficial. Almost any situation can be improved by contributing a positive attitude. They will use this positive example as a training platform when similar situations transpire in adulthood and parenthood.

A teenager's freedom is a necessity, while parental guidance becomes more relaxed. Without proper emotional growth, teenagers' are doomed to fall short of their capabilities and expectations. The parent-teenager relationship, which is created throughout this growth period, will be the platform teenager's adapt to as they become adults.

Any parental behavior observed by a teenager becomes an automatic "green light" to perform the same action.

School

Currently an archaic education platform is responsible for a child's intellectual and social development.

Chapter 1 - Children

Absent of parents and siblings a young child begins that academic and social platform we all know as school. This experience is the first social interaction outside of the child's family and friends. While a child's primary perception of this newly discovered horizon could be one of joy, for some this is quickly dismissed as the results of their academic testing is delivered.

Individual learning curves produce wide gaps in absorption rates and interest levels. Through systematic testing, strengths and weakness are pointed out. These attributes are then summarized in the form of a report card. If a child is graded below average, apprehension and disappointment consume the once proud parents. This shift forever changes the parent-child relationship.

This downgraded perception is generated by the comparison of other children who outperform the "average," creating torment for a lesser-performing child. Letter grades issued on performance promotes disappointment for everyone besides A+ students. (Some of them aren't happy either). For some students, the pace of particular school subjects is presented too rapidly. Young students typically possess an active imagination, which can contribute to additional distractions to the learning process (ADD). When children feel inadequate they can stop trying while drifting into despair or lashing out in frustration.

This condition debilitates social growth and diminishes self-worth, leveraging well-being further from normalcy. The majority of children's' discomfort is generated from negative events that occur throughout their academic career. The personality of a below-average child develops with a sense of inferiority among classmates. This complex causes the student to seek approval from others outside the academic community. These complexes can manifest into a variety of mental deficiencies that stimulate the subconscious mind.

A pecking order is a natural phenomenon that occurs in any group of students that is controlled by academic and self-confidence levels. This order can contribute to an already failing self-image of an underdeveloped student.

A major deficiency in school grading methods is the inability to gauge intelligence. Though grades "bookmark" the current level of aptitude for a given subject at a particular time, the system fails to consider each student individually. Many academically challenged individuals perform very well in their "element" and succeed in developing profitable businesses without an extended education. Less fortunate students can define their talents but fail to convert them into a lifestyle. This condition forces students into disengaging roles that produce frustration. This aggravation can manifest in a student, propelling them into an unsavory existence. Students can then rationalize their degrading acts by internalizing the reassurance that academic communities have bestowed upon them.

Current School System Failures

- Disconnected students.
- School administration salary restrictions
- Underpaid teachers
- Outdated/absent books and study materials
- Diminishing industrial, cultural arts, and sports programs

Current Social Failures

- Dysfunctional-broken family structures
- An overloaded welfare system
- Correctional institutes filled to capacity

Future Education System Objectives

- Advancing an education platform with a "zero" failure rate
- Promoting social networking by demographics and similar interests

- Building student self esteem by reinforcing a positive outlook.
- Increase student participation in advanced subjects
- Promoting personal happiness
- Downsizing school administration
- Tying teacher salaries to performance
- Integrating industrial requirements into an SMS (student management system), enabling employers to process demand modifications and effectively groom the graduating student body to fulfill employment requirements
- Decreasing human suffering and the penitentiary and welfare load

High-energy minds require stimulation to remain interested. Individual academic learning schedules are needed to preserve self-esteem while they educate.

Proposed Updated Education System (PDE Passion Driven Education)

Allowing an education system that jeopardizes a student's possibility for obtaining success both financially and personally is irresponsible. When students apply themselves to a subject and inevitably fall short, it causes a loss of momentum. The "below average" student is yet

Chapter 1 - Children

another degrading classification used commonly among school administrations. One of the most difficult experiences for a student to endure is flunking a class. This unique distinction scars with a transcending self-degradation. While the school system produces successful and unsuccessful students, they all share a common goal: achieving happiness. This happiness is more easily obtainable with a sufficient amount of self-confidence and social interaction.

Every student aspires to a vision of what they would like life to emulate. These aspirations glean a natural momentum that is required to pursue an interest successfully. Once these interests have been identified, the student will gain velocity academically and socially. Today, students live in a world of technology, with information delivered on an integral platform presented by an interactive medium that promotes natural absorption. This medium can be utilized to initiate an individually tailored educational system that monitors and controls subject pace.

Young students will have basic requirement classes currently featured in schools. In addition to this core education, advanced development will include such studies like "Relationships" and "The Value of Love." As a student matures, the school program will scale to present subject material that progress according to developing interests.

Why Our World

All subjects will be non-age/gender specific allowing a student to mature while creating curiosity in classes previously dismissed. Grade levels will be non-existent. Students steadily evolve and learn until they are ready for passage into the workplace. This transition includes an apprentice position supplied by a journeyman, effectively transferring the collective skill and knowledge to the next generation. By referencing a student's academic report, an employer can estimate expected labor output and quality for the chosen trade.

Groups of students will naturally congregate, forming social groups attracted by commonality while unencumbered by academic influence.

Proposed Features

- Initiate an individualized education platform.
- "Fail stop" requires a student to comprehend a subject before advancing.
- System scales rapidly to meet the requirements of a mature student.
- Promotes social networking based on similar interests and geological locations.
- Uses open source coding for economical development.

Chapter 1 - Children

Students learn at their own pace, succeeding every step of the way. Teachers will remotely track work progress while assisting students flagged in the system. A student's login page can feature messages from teachers and parents, along with a calendar of pending tests and events. Based on student performance, PDE will suggest possible fields of employment.

Encouragement toward one of these suggestions will be mandatory, with the exception of the "passion" clause. This clause will allow a choice of an additional option not suggested by PDE.

All students will be monitored for happiness and performance reporting, which will be used as feedback data to help update the PDE program for future generations.

TUH

Acts of violence leave a lasting affect throughout a lifetime, never forgiven or forgotten. Hurting other people's feelings degrades energy, causing negative reactions.

There is no perfect child–all children suffer from underdevelopment in one or more areas. Personal energy is the essence of a child's life. Protecting this energy with education and understanding creates an advantage toward achieving happiness. If a child is forced to perform they will resent it.

A solid family structure is beneficial for receiving experiences from opposing viewpoints. When negative influences are removed from children they are able to grow without restraint. Positive reinforcement provides natural propulsion toward knowledge and self exploration. Children use their parent's energy to evolve; parents should thank their children for raising them.

Chapter 2
LOVE

Definition of love: an unexplained attraction

ENERGY OF LOVE

The energy of love is responsible for every innovation our modern world encompasses. Advancements such as a dishwasher and water heater were conceived to relieve the suffering of a loved one. It's believed that this unique energy defines our human existence. The emotions associated with love are the most intensive feelings a human can experience. When love is shared it advances life energy while providing guidance into maturity. Like an obsession, people are instilled with a need to love that will intensify or diminish throughout their lifetime.

When love begins, it triggers a sense of comfort and happiness, while the loss of love is painful and debilitating. It's difficult to describe the feeling of love unless it's experienced personally–it's beautiful and strange, all at the same time. Love is primarily used for survival, and on advanced levels, it can deliver lifelong happiness. Love's collective energy among many people (friendship) could be vastly underestimated.

The characteristics of love resemble magnetic energy. The natural attraction or repulsion that occurs between two people is the result of unique combinations of their personal energy. As the relationship continues, these magnetic properties adjust to help people adapt to a level of comfort.

Love's "quality" is subject to the maturity of the individuals. Undeveloped people tend to jump into and out of relationships quickly while searching for the next best experience. This disregard for human emotions results in the devastation of unsuspecting participants. It also continually degrades self-worth, causing an inability to love. Residing at the opposite end of the spectrum is a person that maintains a "high quality" love. These people stay committed to their relationships and are deeply hurt when betrayed.

As a young child, many people fall in love with a family pet, stuffed animal, blanket, or toy. This love is usually brief, with the exception of the pet. This relationship represents the first love of a living entity outside the family structure. Pets accept our love and reciprocate by providing affection throughout their lifespan.

Chapter 2 - Love

A primary thought when love is spoken of is two young people being "in love." But this versatile energy is dispersed and applied over many platforms. Successful control of this energy requires in-depth instruction. When love is misused, it causes grief and despair. Actions or thoughts that move a person further away from love generate negative energy, which produces an extended reversal of forward movement.

Love of a Friend

A friendship is a version of love initiated by common interests and compatible personalities. Once a mutual interest in each other has begun, communication and interaction then transpire. Though these friendships are left out of the reproductive cycle, they contribute to a rewarding life experience. As with any relationship, a friendship will fade if not properly maintained with regular communication. It also requires exhibiting a mutual respect for each other's feelings. This form of love allows a friend to come and go within the relationship more freely and with less emotional turmoil than with family relationships.

A person is exposed to many friendship possibilities that occur throughout typical neighborhood and academic settings. All friendships advance life energy through the facilitation of an expanding social platform.

Some of these interactions are discontinued prematurely due to life-path variations. These disconnected relationships retain some value and have the ability to be rekindled at a future date. Friendships are typically easy to maintain, which allows multiple occurrences. Personal energy can be advanced by reconciliation between estranged friends.

Few will be lucky enough to acquire a good friend at an early age; even fewer will maintain this friendship throughout a lifetime. As a popular saying goes, "Whoever has the most stuff wins," but what they should be saying is, "Whoever has the best friend's wins." Any person with at least one good friend is truly rich.

First Love

The first love between two young people is unique and unforgettable. This intense emotion is coupled with a multitude of unfamiliar experiences. Love begins with a mutual interest followed by a dialogue. These discussions are used to help ease discomfort in the preliminary relationship stages. Once a level of comfort is achieved, passion erupts as the relationship is consummated.

When this primal attraction dissipates it signals the beginning of the "work" portion of the relationship

Chapter 2 - Love

which consists of concessions from both parties. The majority of these relationships will fail due to insufficient information about each other. Perfecting the first love into a lasting and pleasurable relationship requires objective observation before the partnership begins.

A person who is considered attractive has an additional responsibility. Because of the way certain people look, they can attract many potential suitors. Due to this abundance, "cute" people can abuse their position by manipulating others. These willing candidates will go to extraordinary lengths to impress someone who seems out of reach. Unfortunately, after these acts are carried out with little to no result, it creates resentment and self-degradation. An attractive person has a responsibility to not disrupt life energy with impure intentions.

"Love at first sight" has been a long-standing phenomenon involving two people who see each other for the first time, and fall in love. Though sheer numbers could substantiate this claim to a certain degree, this affliction produces the highest failure rate among couples.

Once a person's first love has concluded, the intensity of subsequent relationships can be decreased. A person's first love is special, a truly unforgettable experience.

Why Our World

Lovers

Although the journey of love is not easy, having a partner with whom to celebrate triumphs and endure tragedies while raising children is worth the effort. Before love, there is like, a series of encounters are then designed to proliferate the relationship. Once the relationship has progressed to a comfortable level, love initiates. A lasting relationship with adequate happiness levels is dependent on many factors, including the importance of "mood cycle", duration, and intensity. The correlation and compatibility of these cycles dictate relationship harmony. Some people possess an element of sweetness that can offset mood deficiencies. A level of honesty is needed to construct a solid relationship foundation. Once this foundation is compromised with a major mistake, this "seal" of trust is broken. A period of truthfulness is then needed to mend further trust issues.

A mentally healthy relationship relies on the maturity of the individuals involved. A severe problem can cause a relationship to "lock", not allowing either partner to advance their life energy. When these problems occur, a person has one of three options for proceeding.

- Unhappily get through the situation
- Abandon the situation
- Happily get through the situation

Chapter 2 - Love

Only the third choice can bring positive energy back into the relationship.

In some relationships, the two parties encompass opposite energy levels. These opposing energies require each individual to develop or risk failure of the relationship. The more alike these personality energies are, the more enjoyable the relationship will be, the proverbial match made in heaven.

As in any quest, gumption is required for a successful outcome. This fortitude is needed to endure the daily tasks of maintaining a job and home. This strength also comes into play throughout life's natural hardships. A family household requires a level of attention to continue operating successfully. These chores are divided as natural abilities are applied. This division can sometimes generate animosity if the workload is grossly unbalanced.

Disagreements are inevitable and present themselves in every relationship due to varying view points. Typically, hostilities will rise as voices become abrupt while the couple engages in a power struggle. To defuse these situations, at least one person must admit fault. If this condition is allowed to continue without fault, the relationship will suffer.

Some people are bombarded with external information about their relationship from friends and relatives.

While listening to other people's opinions about any given situation is an option, acting on such information can prove to be a mistake. It would be impossible for an outsider to be completely knowledgeable about any relationship outside their own. People should always consider information from others, but make their own decisions.

There is one common element present within all long-term relationships: the ability to make the right decisions. People must be patient and think things through before they act. A long-term relationship will also produce a guarantee that each person in the relationship will change. When these changes occur, new challenges arise to cope with the new dynamic.

Participants in a relationship engage in a daily struggle while wondering if the partnership is worth continuing. These people are usually in the "educational period" of the relationship when mounting frustration creates an unbearable existence.

Once a mutual consensus to divide the relationship has transpired a natural power struggle begins. Confrontation is used as an attempt to preserve the self-confidence of each individual. This struggle includes rights to children and material possessions.

Some divorce attorneys have been known to promote confrontation to leverage revenue and property

Chapter 2 - Love

from the now-broken family. Ironically, the correct way to end a relationship is the way it started: by giving to each other.

When an individual decides to terminate a relationship, it can cause debilitating emotional damage to the partner. These people have no control over the outcome of a relationship choice but are completely affected by it. This condition is especially damaging to an older spouse.

When a relationship has run its course a mourning process transpires, much like a death of a loved one. As this process concludes, a person will explore alternative relationships that could exhibit the same characteristics as their previous encounter, which produces a "rebound" effect. This condition can cause the rationalization required to provide a comfort level needed to expedite the relationship. This natural reaction is to defend against the thought of an internal problem being the cause of the previous relationship failure. This rebound is coupled with the concern that love might not transpire again within their lifetime.

Some people can obtain many possible "life partner" options. These alternative partner choices produce unknown results, which can cause speculation. This assumption is infused with a "fantasy" factor to help make the comparison more provocative. This common condition is known as "the grass is always greener" syndrome. Though some relationships seem stressful, love is an amazingly accurate facilitator when progressing life energy through its process, though it can be occasionally uncomfortable. Only a couple's fortitude can withstand time and progress life energy.

People that are absent of love for a long period of time develop a fear that it may never find them. When people age standards for a partner are lowered and the willingness to settle becomes seemly appropriate. This condition will result in a premature relationship choice that could conclude in disappointment.

Most people's expectations of love have been extinguished if love has been non-existent in their life as they enter old age. These people fantasize about how they would cherish a loving relationship the rest of their life while they envy couples who still do.

Love is a random natural occurrence that cannot be predicted or planned. People who are forced into a relationship are often denied the experience of love.

A relationship can be facilitated by an occasional outing of fun and frolic. These instances should be used sparingly to avoid a crutch that must exist for the relationship to continue.

Chapter 2 - Love

Lovers are never disappointed and always surprised while appreciating the little things. Each person remains neither submissive nor dominant while trying to please each other. Successful implementation of loves energy creates a mutually beneficial and rewarding journey through life.

Couples in love can achieve happiness by focusing on forward movement in their relationship. While love presents many challenges throughout its process, a successful completion of love's journey is revered as angelic.

Love of Family

The birth of a baby is the most beautiful and incredible event that occurs on earth. Parents are instantly consumed with love and feelings of complete togetherness. Relatives and siblings also join the celebration by showering the newborn and parents with love. This new-found affection for the child creates an unbreakable bond that remains throughout a lifetime. As the baby settles into the parents' lives, love grows stronger and more intense while obtaining a new level of happiness.

Mutual love for the child presents an incentive for the parents to perfect their relationship so they can provide a loving, happy home for their infant. Cohabitating in a positive manner also provides an example for children to proliferate into the next generation.

The unique love bond between siblings is created through many years of growing up together. Born into the same family, they are committed to be connected throughout a lifetime. Relationships between siblings share an advantage of maturing in a common living environment that facilitates development.

Every family is presented with multiple choices for any given situation. Problems within the family unit can be caused by different opinions. If an event concludes with unfavorable results hostile emotions can begin. These adverse feelings are generated when one family member is unable to accept the shortcomings of other family members. Relationships between family members must remain "trouble free" to enable positive energy and growth. If strained relationships exist with no attempt at reconciliation, damage to the family results.

If all family members put themselves second instead of first, the family will flourish with love and support. The health of the family unit must be the forethought of each member, while including aspects such as education, family growth, savings, and retirement plans. Failure to do so will result in expectations failing to come to fruition, and family members suffer.

Chapter 2 - Love

LOVE AND HATE

It's possible to hate the one you love. Hatred toward a spouse is the result of a long term resentment generated from perpetual frustration. This occurrence usually develops in the later years of a relationship and is produced due to of the lack of consideration of one partner toward another. This form of "love abuse" from an immature partner can last a lifetime.

Rationalization and ignorance prevent a person from correcting abusive behavior, which can be as subtle as a snide remark or as brutal as an assault. This injustice can repeat itself for years with the abusing spouse unaware of a problem. In obvious episodes of misconduct, an abusing spouse can feel remorse and may go to extraordinary lengths to make it up to the abused partner.

From the perspective of the abuser, the problem that exists within their relationship is barely noticeable. The ability to progress in these deep rooted situations is generally slow and can take years to resolve. Each person holds a unique tolerance to discomfort that affects the duration of the relationship.

Events of abuse are designed to educate the abuser by observing their partners' grief, while suffering remorseful feelings produced by their actions. An abused lover will sometimes stay with an abusive person because they cannot bear the thought of living without love, even if that love is impure.

Love and Death

Upon the death of a loved one, remorse will follow, this is loves promise. This affliction transcends harmonious and estranged relationships alike. The duration and intensity of mourning is equal to the love shared with that person. Feelings of regret provide an extra hurdle to the mourning process.

The emotional pain brought on by mourning is the process of a "living love energy" being transformed into a memory of love. The mourning process serves to eventually alleviate the discomfort of the event.

Bad Love

A person can love two people in the same way at the same time. When natural energies are allowed to unite, love can begin to manifest. Such relationships contradict the natural balance and inhibit the personal growth process. This practice is not widely accepted.

Chapter 2 - Love

It's impossible to love an item that can't reciprocate love. When love is expressed for a material item such as an automobile, the term that should be used to describe the feeling is "desire." This condition exists by anticipating expectations of happiness once a particular object is obtained. An extended anticipation period increases the level of desire. Once an item is obtained, a person's interest for the item might fade as new desires are kindled. This stepped process of desire followed by obtaining material items perceives happiness which is a substitute for the more difficult task of self-improvement. This vicious circle can be conquered only by acknowledging and appreciating current belongings.

Although money cannot buy love, it can provide the opportunity for love. If a person is attracted to money and another person simultaneously has "the money" an opportunity for love may arise that may not have normally transpired. Money becomes a "crutch" that helps the relationship survive. Inevitably, the couple will either succeed or fail in the relationship, with or without money.

The largest travesty love has endured in recent times has been delivered by the media and manufacturing companies. Intertwined in exploiting loves message these companies introduce unrealistic fantasies in an effort to promote sales.

TUH

Due to the absence of education in the proliferation of "love," human suffering continues at an alarming rate. Without proper training, families are doomed to repeat their mistakes in each generation.

The high failure rate of relationships has caused apprehension for many individuals. This skepticism undermines honest attempts at love, inevitably contributing to their relationships demise. For many filling a void of love becomes an obsession. The education of love and it energies can help protect a person's most valuable "first love" while avoiding the regret and life energy disruption that accompanies relationship mistakes.

Imagine a global support system driven by the love of people, contributing talent and labor without anticipation of monetary compensation, teaching the next generation "on the job" and building a positive mindset through enlightenment. Society's elders will be used as a resource by transferring their wisdom to the next generation. The strain and manipulation of money would cease to exist while allowing these newly freed resources to effectively raise the standard of living.

Relationships are a living energy that requires positive reinforcement to stay healthy. By not acknowledging negative aspects, only the positive remains.

Chapter 3
THE EVILS

Greed

Many people's lives are contorted by greed on a daily basis. The obsession of money and the potential happiness it could bring can cause loving parents to work incessantly while watching their family grow up without them. Regardless of consequences, the thought of money can overwhelm the integrity of a person who fails to acknowledge the line between "satisfactory" and "excessive."

People often perform unfair business practices while convincing themselves that "the money is for their family". By charging excessively or shortcutting quality these transactions unjustly remove revenue from another family while creating negative energy for both parties. This compromise is confronted by rationalization and ultimately regret.

There is a profit margin on most products and services. The amount of the profit is a closely guarded secret in many financial transactions. This profit secretly hides the fact that the business is making money above and beyond the actual cost. Increasing or decreasing this margin is the responsibility of the company ownership. This decision is a consideration to the business's sustainability. If a miscalculation of this margin transpires, the jeopardy of the company and its employees ensues. Everyone concerned experiences uncertainty and discomfort if the future of the company is ambiguous. Business is built on "secrets" and how to make money within them.

Occasionally advertisers and manufacturers produce propaganda in the form of products and suggestive ads that are designed to generate revenue with little regard for the people they target. The moral validity of these ambitions degrades society by causing distrust on a large scale.

Historically, companies would abuse employees knowing many people were waiting in line to fill a position that a disgruntled employee might vacate. American labor unions were developed to ensure safety and fair wages for employees by leveraging their work-force while effectively holding the company hostage. Unfortunately, labor unions have added a substantial cost increase that has created an unfair advantage for foreign competitors that are slowly strangling these American companies.

As a natural survival instinct people are attracted to information involving human tragedies. Some news media services display excessive human shortcomings to provide themselves with advertising capabilities (commercials). This industry of "shock and awe" sensationalizes negative human behavior to generate a profit with an unsettling disregard for moral turpitude. This constant barrage of negativity affects anyone who watches.

Our society cannot exist without the monetary compensation system currently in place. Money is the root of all evil, but without cash, life is evil. My father once told me," It's a good business deal if both people felt like they got screwed." If there is a devil, he created the capitalism system.

Earning money will never help a person sustain happiness. People play its game throughout their life, chasing a perceived happiness they never find. A person can be happy at almost any level of existence while enjoying relationships with family and friends. People that value these relationships beyond money represent the truly non-greedy and have mastered a valuable step toward enlightenment.

The most valuable thing anyone can give their family is love. This, in turn, contributes to an enjoyable life; everything else takes care of itself. This often means simply living with less material items.

Greed has slowly destroyed the human experience for many people. Because of greed, a person can become unattached from what's important, love. These people often end up dying alone and un-loved. Greed is the "big winner" for being the "biggest loser." Greed causes more discomfort than all evils combined.

Jealousy

People are familiar with the tag line for "jealousy" as the "the green-eyed monster". This phrase was coined by Shakespeare in *Othello* to describe the feeling of jealously a husband experienced who had caught his wife cheating. The intensity of jealousy is directly related to the amount of love shared. Jealousy can't exist without love.

Jealousy is a natural defense reaction to help thwart the fear of a person betraying love and the discomfort it will bring. Occurrences of jealousy can be created by inconsiderate people who are unable to consider the pain caused by their indiscriminate acts. An overactive imagination produced by an insecure partner can add unfounded turmoil. These conditions slowly erode relationship quality while breeding distrust.

Addiction

Though an addiction can cause negative side effects, it serves as a relieving agent that removes mental or

Chapter 3 - The Evils

physical discomfort. Each addiction is unique to the individual and can consist of a wide variety of experiences. This repetitious occurrence temporarily enhances life's daily experience.

An addiction can easily turn into an obsession that will alter a person's lifestyle. When this lifestyle is removed, it causes discomfort while the person is returning to a "normal" reality. In life's balance, no addiction is healthy, not even an addiction to being healthy. Personal growth is realized in this evil when life is balanced.

Arrogance

Arrogance is used to boost self-image by leveraging money, talent, or intelligence. This self-imposed admiration is required to help boost low self-esteem while degrading the self-worth of others. Receiving gratification from other people is a natural human desire. The lack of patience to receive such compliments breeds resentment, ultimately lowering life energy. Though arrogance shares the similar characteristics as "self-confidence," it holds the distinct attribute of creating rejection. Humility must be exercised while exhibiting superiority to avoid conveying arrogance.

Ignorance

Essentially, there is nothing negative about being unknowledgeable about a particular subject. "Not knowing" simply facilitates the need for more information before confirming a prognosis. Ignorance is exhibited when a person is willing to move forward on a particular event without confirmation using the archetypal "educated guess." The damage of ignorance is multiplied when the condition is applied to personal health issues.

Often a person has reasonable doubt but is confident enough to offer information that may improve the situation by following their advice with the phrase "I think so." This allows an objective discussion to transpire that is required to facilitate further investigation.

Judgmental

The act of being judgmental is a conditioned response developed from past situations that have resulted in a negative outcome. This appearance or action-based emotion has proliferated into almost every aspect of our existence. Though its true people have only one chance to make a first impression, the portrayed assumption is almost always incorrect.

Chapter 3 - The Evils

When people are observed in stressful situations they can be perceived as hostile. In typical situations the same people can be perceived as being normal. Being overly judgmental limits life energy by introducing negative energy.

Lazy

Surprised to see "lazy" as an evil? Virtually every negative human emotion can be attributed to being lazy. The act of being lazy is damaging in itself because it allows a person's sense of responsibility to become relaxed, causing discomfort to others.

The act of being lazy doesn't restrict itself to becoming a "couch potato". A person can be busy but still lazy. These lazy-busy people engage in many senseless activities while neglecting work-related responsibilities.

Deception

When it comes to hurting a person's feelings, deception is at the top of the list. Lies effectively remove the trust element of a relationship while diminishing life energy. Deception defaces the noble notion of truth and, along with greed is one of the simplest evils to correct.

Created to protect the feelings of others, a "white lie" resides in a completely different category than a negatively oriented premeditated lie. A white lie projects a positive energy, created by the consideration of another.

RATIONALIZATION

Rationalization is a combination of laziness and greed. People often try to rationalize immoral behavior by creating an excuse for their action. This self imposed excuse is designed to provide comfort while attempting to offset an injustice designed to supply an ill-gotten gain. This seemingly harmless evil quietly erodes personal growth.

VENGEANCE

A direct result of a personal hardship, vengeance is directed at someone or something that has created a tragedy. This discomfort can convert into rage, which is then directed at the perpetrator. To transcend this evil, the reason behind the unfriendly act must be identified and accepted. Once reconciliation between the two affected parities has transpired, vengeance can be defused, avoiding further retaliation.

Chapter 3 - The Evils

Lack of Appreciation

It's natural to desire a special material item or experience for the people you love. These acts of kindness reward the recipient while enhancing the life experience of the giver. A person who appreciates these good deeds facilitates positive energy. Someone who fails to acknowledge these gifts damages future intentions.

TUH

A company is the sum of its team members that live and die by the devotion to a common cause. When positive thoughts and actions are generated, the company grows while facilitating financial harmony.

Companies and advertisers that practice fair compensation for their goods or services earn nobility and honor from their employees and patrons. Business owners who have a natural compassion for their employees as fellow humans happily succeed.

People have a propensity to allow many evils into their lives, more than they would like to admit. While some of these problems are hereditary, others result from a simple lack of training.

Why Our World

Throughout life's journey, a person will create many discomforts while this basic self-training initiates. The damage of these mistakes affects innocent bystanders who are helpless in the situation. Mistakes will range from minor to extreme and will cause a lifetime of regret.

While materialism has compromised a large portion of the world's population many people are blessed with little. This absence of material items relieves this distraction, leaving them free to experience life's relationships.

Training children about these natural human pitfalls will allow them to create proper practices as they advance their life energy.

Chapter 4
POSITIVE, NEGATIVE, AND BALANCE

Beneficial relationships of family and friends have been a human desire since the beginning of time. Relationships enhance life's experience, while contributing to the advancement of life energy. Since the start of our human existence, a natural connection has facilitated survival through collective intelligence. This knowledge is handed down through each generation while promoting our understanding.

Developing positive behavior patterns is at the core of every person's existence. These patterns develop as absorption rates dictate the ability to change. When people decide they are not satisfied with their current life choices, they sometimes make drastic changes in search of happiness. Once these life-altering changes have occurred these people realize, they are no happier now then they were before the change.

Even though an occupation can be troublesome, it defines the person and provides balance. Once a rigorous work schedule has been performed, amusement can follow.

Dominant and Passive

Dominant behavior exhibited toward an underdeveloped person is a self-promotion tool produced from ignorance and manifests itself in physical or mental capacities.

A dominant person has the upper hand when someone who is passive invites a relationship. A passive person will submit to demands in anticipation of a permanent connection. Overbearing people dictate the mood of the relationship by showcasing their difficulties and triumphs. These acts of domination erode the self-confidence of the person being dominated.

When dominant people exercise humility they advance their life energy by observing the growth of someone passive. When a passive people are allowed to make their own choices, it builds self-esteem. A combination of give and take promotes personal growth by establishing a balance between individual shortcomings and strengths.

Producing a win-lose situation through a game platform promotes self-degradation of the loser while

Chapter 4 - Positive, Negative, and Balance

temporarily boosting self-confidence of the victor. One of the best examples of this condition can be observed at any Little League sport playoff. With anticipation of being victorious, each player enters the field for the game that will decide their fate. Anticipation of a winner builds as the game is played. At the game's conclusion, the victorious team is announced. The winning team responds with cheering, high fives and laughing, while in the loser's dugout there is sadness, as well as feelings of despair and sobbing.

Each of these players engage the game to the best of their ability, but due to varying ability levels and the luck of the game, it forces a favored outcome for half of the competitors. All games are influenced by chance and must produce a loser to artificially boost the winner, which in turn degrades the life energy of the loser. Because competition pushes a person to extreme conditions only those people with the mental capacity to endure failure should participate. Though domination gains the admiration of bystanders, it teaches a person to punish the competition at almost any cost.

Good Practices

People's thoughts and actions control their life energy. These actions have a profound effect on other people's lives. By enabling self-control, a person can avoid behavioral mistakes that needlessly convey negative connotations. A positive mindset combined with patience provides the ability to remove negativity from most situations.

Understanding the benefits of filtering information can promote a positive atmosphere. For instance, a couple purchases a car together that they both admire. At the conclusion of the car's first service, the driver is informed that the car has been in an accident and then was repaired correctly. While conveying this information would properly inform the passenger, it would effectively tarnish the good feelings the car provided. Avoid furnishing negative information unless it positively affects a person's well-being.

In social settings, negative subject matter may be introduced. Such topics can cause emotional distress while collectively removing positive energy from the group. Mastering the art of putting a positive "spin" on subject matter will avoid degrading thoughts while producing an upbeat ambiance.

To receive a compliment from an admired person is a pleasure. This selfless act of generosity elevate the recipients self confidence. Unfortunately, some of these compliments are occasionally used as a tool to degrade a person with the proverbial word, "but." This conjunction is designed to remove the accolade moments after it was bestowed. This style of compliment is "backhanded" and

Chapter 4 - Positive, Negative, and Balance

is shared to artificially elevate the compliment giver while degrading the recipient. For example; a co-worker gives you a compliment on your recent hairstyle, and then follows the gestured with the subtext, "But, that's not the color I would have chosen." This popular occurrence of give and take is fueled by the rationalization of the "false" positive portion of the compliment. A true compliment is a "stand-alone" accolade.

Anytime someone shows interest in a social environment and is excluded, it damages their life energy. This rejection then contributes to their awkwardness. When people express interest, they can offer a unique dynamic which would otherwise not occur without them.

Strangers represent a portion of the interactions a person experiences throughout daily activities. Interacting with these people presents an opportunity to provide a positive experience. These potentially uplifting interactions collectively adjust the energy levels of both parties. Mood cycles have an effect on these interactions that can jeopardize a successful collaboration.

Performing to the best of a person's ability is consistent with self-improvement. Occasionally, doing the right thing can backfire producing a negative outcome. For example; your neighbor offers to help fix a minor plumbing problem you have experienced inside your home. As the neighbor tries to fix the pipe he accidently breaks the pipe completely, causing a hefty repair bill. Circumstances beyond a person's control can yield negative results despite positive efforts. Nevertheless, a person should never use negative results from a good deed to prevent further positive actions.

A person's emotional reaction in any given situation can be judged by a pass or fail grade. These unique occurrences offer a surprise emotion designed to catch a person off-guard. These spontaneous emotional outbursts can cause a person to reflect and grow, while developing proper reactionary emotional skills.

People occasionally require help from someone outside their normal support circle requiring a neighbor or stranger to assist in a task they wouldn't normally perform. Though this task removes attention from the helper's current requirements it builds a personal connection while elevating life energy.

When some people observe a friend or family member's "good fortune," they feel envy or despise that can upset their relationship. This chance discovery is a random occurrence and can be considered only as "luck," while being congratulated and enjoyed.

Regret teaches us that undesirable behavior controls life energy. When self-awareness matures, this "control" becomes an obsession that transforms into a lifestyle.

Chapter 4 - Positive, Negative, and Balance

Karma

The concept of karma, (Originating in ancient India) is a positive and negative energy association based on an "action" or "deed", causing a eternal cycle of cause and effect. Undesirable behavior often leaves a person feeling regretful. These feelings are a product of our human existence, which exhibits natural goodness. This goodness is amplified through a series of communal applications.

When karma is acknowledged, a person experiences an increased desire for improved behavior while simultaneously attempting to correct undesirable demeanor. Expecting immediate coinciding results for a personal positive transformation will produce disappointment. Due to variables in life energy karma will produce sporadic results while positive energy neutralizes negativity. For example; if a mass murder decides he wants to turn over a new leaf, it would take many lifetimes before positive karma would be realized, due to the massive amount of negative energy produced. In preliminary stages of karma awareness uncertain results can create frustration for some people causing a relapse to an underdeveloped self.

A person's life path can present many variations at any given time. When these options present themselves, the results they will produce are unclear. Karma allows people to make a beneficial choice subconsciously, which is usually the first decision that enters their mind. To advance karma, people must be intuitive while acknowledging their inner self.

Karma can't stop unpleasant things from occurring, but over time it can, and will continue to decrease, negative energy.

Karma gives purpose to the human experience while advancing a person's mind by enabling resources to initiate new thought processes. These advances reside exclusively in the subconscious (right brain). Karma is a sense of well-being, an overall indicator of life energy quality that has transcended through many lifetimes.

Mood Cycle

Mood cycles are like belly buttons; everyone has one. Undesirable moods can produce unusual behavioral outbursts while causing irreversible damage to people's relationships. A person's biorhythm cycles are independent of each other and vary in intensity and duration. These cycles exhibit their own independent characteristics and are subject to lifestyle changes.

While a good mood is welcomed, its counterpart is not. Controlling negative moods should become a

Chapter 4 - Positive, Negative, and Balance

priority for preserving a peaceful atmosphere. Various people exhibit subtle mood swings while others have a more difficult task. Having a stable mood enables people to exist while exercising maximum control. Within this control, life energy continues in a stable fashion.

On the opposite end of the scale are people who have massive mood swings, commonly known as bi-polar disorder. These swings produce breathtaking levels of emotion as extreme examples of each variable become apparent. A person with this condition must develop defense mechanisms to help minimize emotional damage. As these tools develop, a positive behavior pattern emerges while building self confidence. A common tool used by a bi-polar person is mental pacification. This distraction allows a person's subconscious mind to work in the background while calculating solutions. Sleep deprivation can also cause enhanced levels of negative emotions.

While recognition of mood patterns is nothing new, a successful definition of individual templates has not been discovered. Old-fashion biorhythm tracking methods calculated a person's birthday coupled with twelve astrological signs to produce a general mood prediction. Successful calculation of these predictions could fine-tune daily expectations. Our modern society has failed to recognize these fortuitous life affirming advantages.

TUH

If the daily labor aspect of life were removed from people's lives while retaining their current lifestyle, temporary happiness would follow. But, eventually many people who are no longer working experience uselessness and boredom. They are then compelled to return to the workforce to enhance their self-worth by helping others.

Each person is unique and must be supported to cultivate a robust society. Every astounding event that has been performed on this earth has been carried out by a normal human.

Chapter 5
THE UNCONSCIOUS MIND

When it comes to thought processes, humans and computers are similar but not the same. Computers have an advantage in the aspect to their ability to produce expansive calculations that would otherwise be impossible for a normal person to conduct. The power of computers continues to expand with a persistent evolution. In 2011, IBM introduced Watson to the world on the popular television show "Jeopardy." This "super computer" is a product of millions of dollars coupled with the most brilliant minds in the field. Though Watson was victorious in the competition against its human competitors, there is one thing Watson will never experience; being human.

Humans are designed with a two part brain, the conscious (left hemisphere) and subconscious (right hemisphere). Though the left brain is logical and accesses memory files much like a computer, the right side of the brain is a little more mysterious. The "right" brain encompasses the production of inspiration, imagination, passion, dreams, involuntary bodily functions, mood, and maturity level.

Though housed in the same environment as its counterpart, this unconscious mind has no motor skills, external sensory inputs, or logical thinking and exists almost completely separate from the conscious mind.

While there is no direct way to communicate with the right brain, it has awareness of environmental surroundings by extrapolating energy provided by left-brain activity. This is accomplished by utilizing an "information bus" called the "corpus callosum," which acts like a toll bridge between the two halves. Communication between these halves can vary depending on mood and environmental conditions. The conscious mind thought process affects the production of inclinations created by the right brain.

If right-brain inclinations are unfulfilled for extended periods of time, it impedes communication effectively removing inspiration and motivation, which is commonly known as depression. Depression is a result of an "asymmetrical" mind, which can be corrected only by restoring balance.

While pharmaceutical companies claim some success in the fight against depression, the placebo effect could be partially responsible. When medications fail, it causes a "backfire," which can increase the feeling of hopelessness. Depression medications might be ineffective due to their inability to work effectively on the right brain.

Chapter 5 - The Unconscious Mind

During the REM (rapid eye movement) portion of sleep, conscious brain activity diminishes, allowing a dream sequence to initiate. Dreams allow the unconscious mind to operate in relative isolation. Dreams articulate scenes that create a "theme" varying in subject matter and intensity. While some dreams exhibit a placid vibrancy, others invoke an intensity that transfers into a person's conscious memory. These dreams can be experienced in black and white or color. This internal observation variance is due to right brain maturity, which is independent of left-brain development levels. Subject matter of a dream can be influenced by recent memory files stored in the conscious mind. While the right brain is naturally luminous, undesirable imagery from the left brain can impede positive functionality.

When a person is subjected to extended sleep deprivation the left brain remains engaged, not allowing the right brain to operate freely, which will cause malfunctions and eventually death.

The right brain holds the key to inspiration and intelligence. Unlocking the problem solving capabilities of the unconscious requires a combination of left-brain stimulus and pacification produced by menial tasks. Within this communication confusion, bits of information are processed to the conscious in the form of an inspiration.

When a person listens to music, the left brain is inputting information that is sensed by the right brain, which translates its rhythm into pleasure.

If the information relationship between the separate brain halves malfunctions, it produces jumbled translations that can lead to schizophrenia.

Animals are created with the distinction of unitizing their complete right brain. This lack of logic enables their inspirational mind to be completely unencumbered.

Happiness

The characteristics of pain and happiness are at opposite ends of the scale. Pain and anger tend to ramp up quickly, while happiness is more of a passive objective that must be cultivated over many years.

Emotional discomfort and happiness define people's existence while affecting their life energy. Each of these conditions is a product of environment and emotional outlook, which creates the duration for each condition.

A common misconception on the pilgrimage to happiness is the desire for extravagant material items.

Chapter 5 - The Unconscious Mind

Though these items can help a person enjoy life with loved ones by providing experiences otherwise not found without money, these experiences are absent of substance unless shared. Only after obtaining everything a person could want does the realization come to fruition, life was better before the quest for material items began.

Throughout society, outdoing coworkers, friends, neighbors, and family has become an epidemic. This competition is expedited by the assumption that once victorious, happiness will follow. These pointless battles of collecting material items have camouflaged behavior required to achieve happiness while producing irreparable financial casualties.

Incremental advancements in people's status improve their social position while boosting perceived opinions among peers. This persona is a superficial perception that doesn't necessarily correlate to a level of happiness.

Occasionally, a person's home or work environment can be drastically altered for the worse. These new changes are strenuous while being introduced into an unfamiliar lifestyle. Along with this new lifestyle, a degraded self-image can follow which is facilitated by skepticism from peers, friends, and family. This downgrade is caused by a failure to acknowledge life assets unless accompanied by tangible items.

Major life changes inevitably pull a person in a new direction. The amount of discomfort experienced is equal to reluctance to accept the change. This new life path directs a person regardless of monetary compensation. These environmental changes are a normal evolutionary occurrence and should not be taken personally. This new platform expedites the advancement of life energy.

Traumatic events have a devastating effect on a person's life. Family and friends provide love and support to convey their sorrow for the situation. These people act as a grounding agent which extracts a portion of the negative energy away from the afflicted person. This allows a person in this situation to regain their life energy momentum. Without this sympathy a person can be engulfed by negativity and drift into despair.

Everybody has a degree of regret present in their lives. It's impossible to be alive and experience absolutely no regret. Avoiding regretful events becomes apparent at adolescence with the recognition of hurt feelings of another person. This lifelong learning process is designed to enlighten while avoiding actions that will yield negative results. Controlling these compunctious acts can be difficult due to the unexpected nature of random situations. Remorseful acts produce negative energy, which imbeds itself into deep conscious memory that can be recalled at any time in full validity. A concerted effort is

Chapter 5 - The Unconscious Mind

needed to stem remorseful acts to minimize life-energy damage. Controlling emotional pain is instrumental in the successful achievement of happiness.

A person's happiness level is directly related to the satisfaction of the unconscious mind.

Anger

Anger is traditionally generated by one of three phenomena: fear, experiencing an undesirable event, or betrayal from a loved one. Humans have the natural ability to recognize and react to negative events. This anger emotion creates an uncomfortable feeling that produces rage, which has contributed to human survival. By informing family and friends of a situation, it reduces anger's side effects. These confessions effectively remove a portion of the negative energy created. This emotional safety net is designed to buffer extreme conditions that would otherwise cause sociological damage.

The transition between fear and anger can be instantaneous. The inconsistency with which an anger event occurs adds difficulty in predicting, which causes a person to be caught off-guard. Acts of violence can often accompany anger which signifies an escalation of reluctance for a situation. Collateral damage from unwarranted acts of anger can motivate a person's control to minimize casualties.

Anger can be defused only by communication coupled with the fortitude to "stay in control" through emotions duration. Defusing anger by successfully concluding an incident serves as a tool to achieve personal growth.

TUH

The effects of opposing positive and negative energies on a person are dramatic. For instance, imagine someone who observes life with a positive attitude despite negative events. This person will enjoy their life journey while spreading positive energy to others.

On the flip side, imagine someone who lives life in the complete opposite manner, observing events in a negative light while affecting others. This negative existence creates very little happiness while attracting undesirable events. These are completely different types of people going in opposite directions, though their material lifestyles are similar.

Narcissism causes wide-spread unhappiness because it makes people reluctant to consider the happiness of people around them. True happiness can be achieved only when everybody in a person's life is happy.

Chapter 5 - The Unconscious Mind

Happiness is achieved on a daily basis by converting negative energy into positive. Don't obsess over things you can't change; everything happens for a reason. Help where you can and enjoy life. Happiness consists of harmonizing experiences with many growth stops along the way.

Happiness cannot exist, without pain.

Chapter 6
UNIVERSE, TIME, AND ENERGY

Positive thought processes produced by the mind will expel the body's negative energy. The volume of thoughts produced is equal to the amount of energy consumed. People possess a unique energy level that develops throughout their lifetime. When a person lives with purpose and tenacity it increases the body's usage, which burns fuel. Advancing life energy is achieved by promoting a positive work and home environment while improving personal relationships and advocating physical activities.

Some societies believe a person's mood is controlled by celestial cycles and the gravitational energy provided by the earth's relationship to the stars and planets in our universe. Deciphering these positional relationships and calculating individual results which create a pattern can take years. A predicable mood cycle provides value by enlightening a person with improved awareness. Comprehension of these cycles is complicated by peripheral forces not related to planet location such as environmental conditions.

The energy of "happiness" and "karma" are universal human desires which develop a state of mind over a life-long pilgrimage. When a tragedy occurs, people are compelled to assist with the energy known as "compassion."

The rules of time and energy are intriguing; each is unique in scope and usability. Our universe presents an endless field of possibilities that spark the imagination of anyone that gazes into the cosmos on a star-washed night.

Universe

Everything in existence must adhere to the guidelines of time, space, and energy. Space serves as a suspension agent on the interior of the universe where galaxies contain "energy mass" ($E=mc^2$).

Since the beginning, people have been investigating the universe while searching for clues to our origin. Through observation, ancient astronomers created a basic "road map" that included twelve star constellations.

Modern society once believed that travel into space would yield information that would benefit all mankind. Since then, worldwide space programs have produced

Chapter 6 - Universe, Time, and Energy

spacecrafts that perform various functions. Currently the universe is studied with an urgent passion using computerized structures that house colossal telescopes. These programs gather data that are stored and ready to be analyzed by scholars, teachers, and students alike.

Space exploration and observation programs have used vast amounts of natural resources, including millions of hours from field professionals. This observation and "big journey" into space is largely a disappointment with no life-confirming answers to report. Developing the ability to observe life on a planet outside our solar system by modern methods is extremely remote.

The question is, for all the effort that has been expended in the exploration of the universe, why is so little information returned? Space exploration was like being excited about a "road trip" which is generated by the anticipation of discovery. Once the destination has been reached, interest is experienced, but no real answers are found.

Time

On earth, the mechanical measurement of time remains a constant with very little deviation. Though living in the fabric of time is a mandatory requirement of every living thing, little is known about this medium other than the fact that it moves forward.

There are several everyday occurrences in which the "manipulation" of the perception of time is exhibited. The perception of time can be distorted by desirable and undesirable situations. When people fall asleep they fade out of consciousness, causing the acknowledgment of passing time to become contorted.

One of the most impressive displays of "fabric" manipulation involves removing people from the continuum temporarily and then reinserting them at a later time. These instances occur daily in local hospitals. Prior to an operation, an anesthesiologist administers a drug that renders a person unconscious to avoid discomfort. These drugs are then monitored to ensure that the patient maintains a prescribed level of medicine in their bloodstream.

This state of induced unconsciousness is not a "sleep" state (the person cannot be awakened). The administered anesthesia effectively leverages life energy away from the body and out of the time continuum. This person is absent of almost all thought processes, which includes any recollection of time passing. During this unconscious state, a person's life energy is non-existent.

At the conclusion of the procedure, the patient's body is allowed to recover, which re-activates the life energy back into existence and into the current time continuum. The acceleration into the current time

Chapter 6 - Universe, Time, and Energy

continuum can cause motion sickness. The severity of the nausea is related to the duration of the unconscious state.

Though the fabric of time presents many standard variables, it also offers an equal amount of mystery.

Energy

Positive and negative energy is the basis on which all creation is constructed. These opposites represent the presence of time as well as the absence of time, like magnetic fields. This theory is experienced by allowing two magnets to naturally draw themselves together, and when reversed they repel. (Magnetic fields)

More than just "magnetism" this action represents "matter" existing and then not, simultaneously (a common quantum physics assumption). This principle is the essence of electricity, which operates on the same platform. Collectively, all elements of energy and mass create the universe, which must conform to the rules of existence and non-existence.

Through trillions of years, every particle of energy in our galaxy migrates to the center of the Milky Way, where it's consumed into "Sagittarius A" (a massive black hole) that exists as the "absence of time." Once these elements enter the "time void," they are simultaneously transported back into the time continuum at the outer edge of the galaxy, where energy mass is reconfigured and reborn as new a planet, star or solar system. Small asteroids and other space debris are the result of this process. As a planet, star, or solar system is pulled closer to the Milky Way, the fabric of time is consumed at a more rapid pace. There are countless galaxies contained within the universe.

Electromagnetism is generated by the same positive and negative components used in a typical electrical application. Each "mass" in the universe possess a unique magnetic state which in turn is used to suspend a planet, star or solar system in a particular location in the galaxy. By comparison, the mass of a planet, star or solar system and force confining them to their orbit or placement is feeble. These massive fields of energy create flash holes which represent alternating current and are capable of propelling energy between solar systems and planets inside a galaxy.

A person's mind is efficient in creating energies qualified to heal imperfections in the body. Primitive cultures depend almost completely on these healing energies. Tribe members use local plants and other ingredients infused with positive energy to help generate momentum in the healing process. Because this method is not 100 percent effective, it has drawn skepticism and

Chapter 6 - Universe, Time, and Energy

controversy throughout western culture. The lack of research in perfecting these processes has led to the advancement of traditional chemical treatments.

The term "in the zone" is a phenomenon referred to when a person appears to have super-human strength or talent. These seemingly impossible tasks is the result of the right brain being allowed to materialize through the conscious mind (left brain). Once an event initiates, it can become more extraordinary by allowing the right brain function and assume complete control. While in complete right brain mode the conscious mind is absent making recollection of the event difficult. This extraordinary energy is available to anyone that can activate their right brain function.

Though the right brain is capable of extraordinary accomplishments most activities are subtle. For example, a person is looking over a crowded room, and suddenly her eyes are drawn to a person in the crowd looking right at her. This uncontrollable connection is produced by a reaction created subconsciously in both people.

At gatherings such as a party, energies comingle, creating a multi level moxie impossible to achieve individually. This positive energy cannot be forced into a particular social event. It can be achieved only if the participants allow such energy.

Our current society's comprehension of the right brain and its capabilities is in the infantile stages. Humans are the only species that possess the ability to individually engage either right or left brains. Animals are almost completely right brained so they communicate and react without apprehension by interpreting energies in their vicinity.

Dogs are dependent on their ability to sniff an item of clothing to help seek its owner, even from miles away. Though a dog's smelling capabilities are far greater than a human's this seemingly impossible task is performed with hyper sensitivity to energy, and scent.

Much like humans, pets can have inherent personalities that can complement or repel their owner. These innocent minds "see" life energy through the use of their right brain and react accordingly. Animals remain in this innocent state and seek positive energy stimulation throughout their lives.

The human body is a support system that contains life energy. This body is a chemically based, bio-fuel converting, electro impulse machine controlled by the brain.

Energies support and control every aspect of a person's life. While some energy is subtle, others types of energy have a very noticeable effect.

Chapter 6 - Universe, Time, and Energy

TUH

Problem solving has been a civilization's nemesis since the beginning.

Time forces everything in the universe to change. These changes occur because energy cannot stay the same and survive.

The creation of the universe is irrelevant. The importance of the universe is realized in the comprehension of the energies its galaxies encompass.

Knowledge is gained from the universe by attracting positive energy. This attraction is created by clearing your thoughts while gazing into a clear night sky. This positive action will invite energy into a person's right-brain function in the form of an inspiration.

Happiness and time are closely related. A person's happiness must be obtained for each second of time. This is difficult because most people are looking forward to their next thought or action. To experience time with happiness people must be capable of appreciating their current surroundings. If this state of mind is unsuccessful, happiness cannot transpire.

We feel the fabric of time throughout the day, like a gentle blanket continually pulled across our bodies, always moving. This "medium" allows a person to learn how to advance life energy after regretful actions, while obtaining joy when conscious acts of goodness are performed. These actions are designed to teach by self-reflection while perfecting positive actions. Without time the ability to increase life energy would be impossible.

Wherever positive energy thrives, negative energy will be close by, naturally attracted to each other. This negative energy can arrive in obvious and seemingly innocent forms alike.

A person's existence is defined by the beginning and ending of each rotation of the earth. Yet the time span of our human existence is so diminutive it's almost immeasurable compared to the life span of the universe.

Modern society has traveled into and magnified the cosmos. This direction has produced no "big picture" results. Rather than looking at the universe as a complicated device that is seemingly impossible to understand, simply observe the cosmos as the multi-layered energy platform that it is.

Planet earth supplies a life-supporting condition that drives human evolution. The possibility of these conditions occurring elsewhere in the universe is inevitable.

Chapter 7
DEATH AND REBIRTH

LIFE ENERGY

Life and death represent the two separate phases of a person's life energy: existence and non-existence. These phases reside at the opposite ends of the spectrum and exhibit completely different applications. While living, a person's life energy has the opportunity to be changed. In death, the life energy is the result of those changes.

Memories of regretful incidences resurface when a person is close to death or has had a near-death experience. A desperate compulsion to connect with estranged loved ones is an attempt to gain positive energy. Regretful actions imbed themselves in a person's memory to accentuate their importance. The accumulation of good and bad memories creates a person's life energy.

Subject to a person's thoughts and actions, life's energy contains many characteristics of electricity that advance or decline with each instance. This energy-level progression is similar to traveling on a large staircase, each stride leading to the next, ascending or descending. Without forward direction, life energy becomes stagnant, which causes a melancholy state.

Efforts to recreate life have been futile while the origin of life energy remains an enigma. By using a live tissue sample, scientists have been successful in perfecting a cell reproduction cloning process. But this process builds on an existing life platform and does not recreate life.

Cloning a fully fledged human presents a fundamental problem. Although it's possible to create a human body, it would lack a unique life energy which is available only through viable reproduction methods. Due to the absence of a right-brain entity, this new human will lack coherency. This abnormal condition would be difficult to detect in animal cloning due to the absence of a logical mind.

Modern science has been unsuccessful in substantiating proof of an "afterlife," which has produced skepticism and a wide variety of interpretation. This skepticism is divided into three main categories: rebirth, divine destination, or elimination.

Death

Life energy, once in existence, is never lost or dissolved. Life and death exist as completely different

Chapter 7 - Death and Rebirth

energies, negative and positive, time and the absence of it. The "fabric of time" only exists when a person is alive. When people close their eyes for the last time and death overcomes their body, the actual "fabric of time" falls away, effectively separating their life energy from the time continuum.

This life-energy transformation follows the same principles as magnetism. When people are "living," their energy is charged, holding their "life" inside their body. When people die their life energy instantly reverses repelling the energy away from earth and out of the time continuum. Again, this mechanical exhibition of energy (matter) existence and nonexistence is a common quantum physics assumption.

This life energy transfer causes the information stored in the left brain (conscious mind) to be stripped away, while leaving the right brain energy (matter) intact.

When a person is near death they sometimes experience themselves floating over their body. This effect is the result of their life energy being held in "transition" between the universe pulling them into their next life and the current body struggling to hold on. The life energy is pulled back into their body if normal operating functions resume within a short amount of time.

When a loved one dies, a mourning process is experienced which represents "love energy" being transformed into a passive state (love lost).

Rebirth

While in the absence of time state (non-existence), a person's life energy is subject to re-entry protocol. When re-born, a person's life energy is reversed and pulled back into the time continuum and back into existence as their "new life" birth is completed. This complete process occurs very quickly much like a flash of light, despite the amount of time that has passed in the physical world. Remorse from loved ones introduces additional demands, which can affect destination.

This dramatic re-entrance into the current world is accompanied by "extreme momentum" while the reintroduction of the time continuum occurs. An infant is born almost exclusively with right brain capabilities which nullify the effects of re-entry (motion sickness).

An unborn baby is a biological cell formation inside the mother's uterus. As a result of the birth process, life energy enters an infant's body only when it's able to support a "life soul" which usually occurs just outside the womb.

Chapter 7 - Death and Rebirth

Life energy can be transferred only to a life-sustaining body. An infant's right brain functionality enables involuntary actions such as random movements, breast feeding, burping and crying. As the left brain matures it begins to store memory files which initiate coherency.

When an infant is born, it represents three independent life energies: mother, father, and the individual. Though an individual is at the core of this life essence the mother and father play a role in affecting their child's personality. In general, a first born son will have more of his mother's characteristics than his father's, with just the opposite scenario for a daughter. As a second, third, and fourth child is added, the condition loses intensity, allowing future infants to arrive with less parental influences.

When a baby is born, an "automatic love" is shared among family and friends this unconditional joy is "love recaptured."

A person's talent is divided into two separate categories: educational and natural. Educational talent is logical, (left brain) structured and obtained by hours of studying a particular subject. Natural talent is the complete opposite and developed by the right brain which stores passionate characteristics. This natural passion is carried continuously and developed throughout each lifetime.

The content of a REM dream can control a person's mood. These dreams are comingled with fantasy and desire assembled from conscious images and feelings. Though most dreams are recognizable, some dreams can exhibit unfamiliar scenery. These unfamiliar dream elements are a product of right-brain inclinations stored throughout many lifetimes.

Throughout many "lifetimes" people experience both male and female life forms. This gender alternation is influenced by aggressive and passionate energy levels. These fluctuations can become diluted, causing a female to have male tendencies with the opposite effect for males.

TUH

All life forms expel their life energy at the time of their death; the energy is then reinserted when required.

A miracle of life, an infant is created by opposite sexes. Modern science offers no explanations for the genesis of the actual person inhabiting the body.

Love and remorse are the prevailing energies that guide a person's life energy to a particular family throughout the rebirth process. When people experiences the death of a loved one they are involuntarily forced through

Chapter 7 - Death and Rebirth

the various stages of the mourning process. Once these stages have been completed a renewed appreciation for their own life and the possibility it holds begins.

When people die without love they subject themselves to a random rebirth that will accommodate their life energy. Once reborn into a non-loving family, an appreciation for love is accentuated. These people become extraordinary family members due to their profound benevolence for the loved ones in their life.

Occasionally a person near death will see or feel deceased loved ones waiting for them. These are the life energies that are ready to love them in their new life.

The most valuable thing a person can leave behind is a part of themselves in the hearts of loved ones.

Chapter 8
THE ANCIENT EGYPTIANS

It has been suggested that humans have "simply" evolved from another species or that we were "blessed" to earth by a religious event. The origin of man's creation on this earth seems ambiguous because a clear answer hasn't been presented that is even remotely believable. A trustworthy solution would generate commonality for humanity.

Exploration through this chapter begins with a question: How did the first human arrive on this earth? Additionally, is it possible for humans to occupy additional planets elsewhere in the universe?

Within the duration of any large number scenario, such as the human existence on earth, anomalies occur that yield extreme results in both intelligent and ignorant realms. Due to the absence of successful information storage media many extraordinary events have occurred on earth that we have no record of.

Why Our World

Due to misinterpretation of the information and structures found in Egypt, the controversial "Great Egyptians" are generally misunderstood by modern society. A popular perception of these Egyptians is one of an overbearing, sadistic people that used force and slavery to fabricate their monuments and buildings. With many objects created from solid gold, the Egyptians are famous for their wealth and greed.

Though modern science has sifted through the remains, which have produced various opinions of the Egyptian civilization lifestyle, it's difficult to obtain an in-depth understanding of their personal energy, intelligence, and happiness level. Modern science has also failed to explain the purpose the Egyptian structures, monuments, and obsessions.

The ancient Egyptian societies were highly advanced and extremely cultured. These societies were divided into two similar civilizations by a great flood. The first Egyptian kingdom existed in a "Golden Age" (10,500 BC). This advanced civilization constructed four monolithic pyramids and a great sphinx on the Giza Plains.

Historians have traditionally dated the ancient Egyptian society to have begun around 3150 BC and concluded about 30 BC. New evidence and observations have led experts to agree that the pyramids and the great sphinx are from an earlier time. Even ancient pharaohs,

Chapter 8 - The Ancient Egyptians

kings, and philosophers such as Plato spoke of civilizations much grander than their own and referred to a Golden Age of existence.

The crowning achievement and the peak of both Egyptian civilizations were realized in the age of the constellation Leo, at the time of King Osiris with the completion of the third great pyramid and sphinx. (10,500 BC).

Later, the traditional Egyptians' (3150 BC to 30 BC) attempted to re-create the Golden Age Egyptian civilization, but the inability to achieve perfection affected every aspect of their daily living produced mental instability. These impurities led to failed building techniques, which ultimately caused the collapse of the Egyptian society.

These "traditional" Egyptians encompassed many of the teachings of the Golden Age Egyptians with one major exception. Through the next few paragraphs, the mysteries of these Egyptians will unfold, divulging a story of the greatest civilization on earth.

Intelligence

Modern structures have the distinct attribute of an explainable construction process. This statement is not true for the pyramids of Egypt, in both purpose and design. Beyond the physical attributes of the pyramids is the accuracy level and building material used in their construction. Today it would be difficult to duplicate these monuments created by the Egyptians, even with the assistance of heavy building equipment such as a crane.

Ancient Egyptians developed and retained an acute understanding of universe, mathematics, and energy far beyond the comprehension of today's great thinkers. This advanced level of expertise was evolved through years of cultivating positive life energy and expanding subconscious awareness through many generations.

Enabling right brain functionality by altering the conscious mind was an important objective. This was facilitated by deflating a person's conscious mind functionality.

Encompassed within the ancient Egyptian philosophy were astronomers, architects, engineers, craftsman, and visionaries who helped create massive statues, buildings, and monuments.

Egyptians used energy from celestial phenomena by celebrating events such as the rising and setting of the sun. Special homage was given to the summer and winter solstices, along with the spring and fall equinox.

The Egyptian calendar was a multi purpose creation designed to observe the earth's location in the universe

Chapter 8 - The Ancient Egyptians

by identifying twelve groups of stars (the zodiac) called "constellations." This technology was used to map the universe using a complex mathematical methodology to discover additional solar systems. The Mayan calendar was created around the same time as the Egyptian calendar and shares common attributes.

Egyptian Calendar

Not only was this information used to pinpoint the location of the pyramids: it was used to predict individual mood cycles, which would present opportunities that could yield optimum results for particular situations such as falling in love. All aspects of the Egyptian lifestyle were controlled by this calendar, which included the prediction of a new beginning.

Additional advancements included controlling electrical energy while encompassing several of its uses such as illumination and auto-catalytic plating.

ELECTRIC LIGHT

Positive life energy cultivation included an in-depth understanding of the human experience. Comprehension of this development was used to produce advancements required to achieve their objectives.

ANCIENT EGYPTIANS

As basic communication skills mature adolescent Egyptians were instructed about the importance of various energies associated with basic human feelings. The diverse energy of love and its many variations was integral throughout the education process. Childhood activities were designed to be all-inclusive, while academics were

Chapter 8 - The Ancient Egyptians

conducted in a completely positive atmosphere. If an activity produced a negative outcome for one or more of the participants, it was discarded.

Throughout a child's learning process, undesirable emotional situations would naturally arise. This normal process varied in severity and was used to purge negative energy from a past life. These situations were supervised by parents, teachers, and elders, who provided enlightenment that facilitated mental growth. Mood cycles were monitored to control undesirable results in life-changing situations. A child's self-confidence was considered a precious resource. Primary educational materials were focused on a lifelong quest to improve life energy.

Educational subjects were divided into groups that anyone could participate in. The subjects included personal energy development, astronomy, mathematics, and architecture.

Students that were interested in a particular subject, naturally excelled. By adjusting a curriculum to fit the individual, these talents were optimized and skewed toward a particular field of work. Once in the workplace, the education process continued by using hands-on training methods while sharing the collective wisdom of coworkers. Positive human attributes were encouraged with an emphasis on future lifetimes.

Social acceptance was gained through appreciation for any task performed with passion. Tools provided assistance in laborious activities. When used, these tools were infused with the energy of a person's usefulness. It was common to be buried with these items serving as an influence into the next lifetime.

Portraits of "Egyptian pharaohs" exhibit peace and tranquility. This peace was represented by a neutral or slightly upbeat theme that illustrated mental balance. Many gladiators were depicted later in history from civilizations such as the Roman Empire. Documentation of such violence was absent in the time period of the ancient Egyptians.

KING - PHARAOH

Egyptians acquired an acute understanding of the aspects in our world such as the sun, earth, life, and universe while existing within the rules that encompassed them. The willingness to perform manual labor was in direct relation to their desire to advance personal energy.

Profuse attention to energy enabled right-brain functions, which accelerated intelligence levels. The ability to graduate through each level of humanity was the basis on which a person was judged. Honest admiration was used to "filter" leaders, which then formed an administration sector. From this group of people a king or pharaoh was chosen. This appointment could transcend through several lifetimes.

NEFERTITI, WIFE OF PHARAOH AKHENATEN

The bust of Nefertiti, who was the wife of Pharaoh Akhenaten, exhibits an obvious distinction between the right and left brain. These types of head-gear were common and were used to represent the awareness of distinctive brain functions.

The halo used today as an advanced sign of decency and spirituality, was featured in many Egyptian depictions and is the first recorded instance of such a concept.

MUSIC AND CELEBRATION

Music and alcohol were used to stimulate brain functions while connecting energies between people. Among its many uses, music would also create a festive atmosphere at social gatherings, which promoted unique

Chapter 8 - The Ancient Egyptians

group energy dynamics. Performed regularly, music and dance inspired subconscious exercises, which were designed to nurture right-brain activity.

Pharaoh Shown
Holding the
"Key of Life"
and "Energy Rod"

Make-up and costumes were used to reflect a connection that characterized the right brain functionality of various animals. Egyptians admired the right-brain function of animals, which act purely on impulse. Human development of a "reactionary intelligence" was also at the forefront of their studies.

Particular animals such as canines and felines responded to the intense "love energy" the Egyptians provided, which converted them into domestication. This transformation populated future generations of these wild animal "hybrids" which are enjoyed as household pets today.

Felines are equipped with an ability to see the blue end of the light spectrum and the energy it contains. Egyptians could have used this insight to determine the potential love partners of young adults.

Once a love partnership had been established a couple would embark upon a survival adventure. This daunting experience established a base relationship that was facilitated by hardship. At the conclusion of the training, an "energy bonding ceremony" would commence, conducted by a curator. The new couple would then consummate their relationship and begin their new family.

Medical problems consisted primarily of broken bones and lacerations which were remedied by many of the same methods used today. An elevated mental status enhanced immune systems which resisted disease and

Chapter 8 - The Ancient Egyptians

infection. Excellent health conditions were also attributed to wholesome food production and preparation.

Upper-level management would interact with a main counsel who organized, designed, and executed their aspirations. Workers were divided into clusters controlled by a multi layer management system. A group of people called "scribes" were in charge of tracking family living necessities and calculating future cultivation and livestock requirements.

When a hostile situation occurred, people in the immediate area would intervene to help influence the outcome. To protect against unfriendly intruders and wildlife, a group of men maintained the society's perimeter equipped with weapons that could apply force when needed to maintain order.

Improving personal energy was a lifelong theme that was methodically practiced. The aggregate severity of a person's infractions accrued throughout a lifetime warranted (by choice) a life energy "reboot" which consisted of a ritual of death with appropriate mourning of loved ones. This death and re-birth production would help guide a person's life energy to be reborn into the original family. This method cleanses a person's left-brain activity effectively removing all memories and allowing the right brain energy to continue into a new life.

NARMER PALETTE

Illustration of the "cleansing" ritual is featured on the Narmer Palette (right). The left panel illustrates control over the mind through death and rebirth. This transition into a new life, though difficult, produced an improved version of that person. An intricate system was used to "track" life energies and their eventual rebirth. Once in transition, a person's skull or mummy was retained by love ones to help attract the returning life energy.

Many Egyptian depictions feature different size people. This was used to advertise the life energy development stage of a particular aspect.

The objective of the Egyptians was developing and controlling conscious and subconscious energy. Chosen by a hierarchy, a king or pharaoh was considered the most mentally advanced. These candidates were not limited by age or gender. These passive rulers were used as a focal point designed to collectively magnify the energy from their society. Absent of controversy, this appointment unlocked extraordinary mental capabilities while accelerating life energy. The pharaoh would then feedback this energy throughout society.

These masters of life energy were necessary for guidance in the development of their societies.

Pharaoh

A "tail" of a gold metal thatch was hung at ground level acted as a conductor to the earth, facilitating the removal of negative energy. A "spiral" symbol featured in Egyptian portraits represents a specific order sequence in which life energies could be accepted back into the world.

DOUBLE
CROWN
PHARAOH

Material items were bestowed onto the pharaoh to serve as a gift that would connect life energies. Illustrations of this connection were shown as a halo or headdress of energy on or slightly above the pharaoh's head. Evidence of this energy connection is also observed in the clothing, which was attracted to a magnetic "power rod" commonly associated with pharaoh's.

No person suffered from hunger or loneliness. Everyone who desired the Egyptian way of life was included and integrated into their working society. People interacted in social development areas were family units depended on each other for survival. Individual talents

Chapter 8 - The Ancient Egyptians

didn't change a person's classification, as everyone acknowledged themselves as equals. The value of monetary items such as food, building materials, artwork, metals, and gems was non-existent.

The majority of ancient Egyptians believed in this advanced focus. A minority group of underdeveloped people couldn't grasp the progressive Egyptian teachings and mindset. This contradiction produced different opinions on the purpose of their human existence.

Insubordination among management and work crew personnel would prove to be detrimental to construction projects. While attempting to duplicate the building and mental perfection of the "Golden Age Egyptians" (10,500 BC) the "traditional Egyptians" (3150 BC to 30 BC) built more than one hundred pyramids. Deficiencies in mental capabilities caused failed building techniques which produced imperfections in many of these ill-fated structures. Throughout this ancient time period, various civilizations around the world were compelled to construct a variation of the four great pyramids. Many of these pyramids had no practical use. Due to this comprehension gap, the traditional Egyptians never realized the ultimate use of pyramid building.

The Great Pyramids of Giza were never entered by the traditional ancient Egyptians. The hidden entrance into the first great pyramid was not discovered until 820 AD.

Why Our World

The Golden Age of Osiris

Osiris was the last king of Egypt (Golden Age 10,500 BC – illustrated through the star constellation Orion) and possessed the most advanced life energy in their society.

Osiris and the Golden Age Egyptians observed the universe through mathematics while witnessing a specific order in which life-bearing planets should be inhabited. These Egyptians studied the universe in all directions (isotropy) and from every location (homogeneity).

The Family of Osiris

(Osiris on a lapis lazuli pillar in the middle, flanked by Horus on the left and Isis on the right.)

Positive actions and limited distractions throughout society relieved the Egyptians subconscious, which enabled improved mental functionality. This elevation was used to discover concise directions in human evolution pertaining to the repopulation of additional life supporting-planets.

Chapter 8 - The Ancient Egyptians

By studying star orientation patterns, the Egyptians discovered a set of "target" adolescent life sustaining planets that would serve as their objectives.

The Egyptian subconscious produced problem solving not rendered from the conscious mind. This discovery process included a method of shutting down the left-brain function while allowing the right brain to flourish. While in this mind-altered state, the fabric of time was controlled in combination with the earth's rotation resulting in a "life energy tracer". This "tracer" would produce a "snap-shot" that was used to convey of the level of life energy present on an objective planet. The rotation of the objective planet would propel the returning energy to the recipient. The information gathered contained specifics needed to expand the "master equation." Once this objective was finalized, construction designs commenced for the "machine" that would enable their journey.

Great Pyramid of Giza
(Golden Age, − 10,500 BC).

The mathematical implications for the project were staggering. Ideas and equations were considered from people outside the normal mathematician realm. Structurally, the pyramid designs were created with astonishing accuracy and benevolence, combining mass with height. This bulk design was used to confine energy while allowing existence above the earth's surface which enabled separation from the earth's mass.

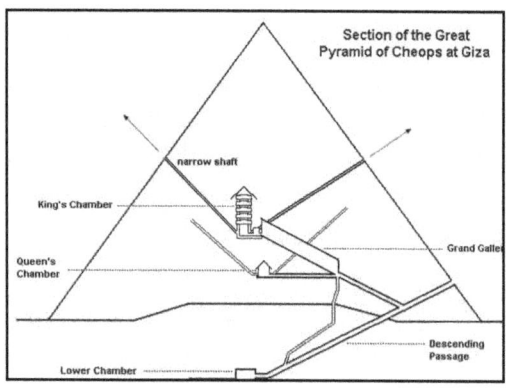

GREAT PYRAMID
INTERIOR DIAGRAM

Initially, the room historians classified as the "queens chamber" and the adjacent partially completed propulsion tubes (classically referred to as "air vents") were part of the pyramid's primary design. This original architecture was scrubbed and modified to include the construction of a "king's chamber," which was located higher and slightly offset to execute a final update and conclusion to the project objective.

Chapter 8 - The Ancient Egyptians

Once the pyramid was completed and in alignment with the "coordinate destination," the king entered the "king's chamber," where the prophecy was realized by releasing his "life energy" (death) from the time continuum. The pyramid would then contain and compress the life energy creating an energy projectile which was then dispatched through one of the propulsion shafts.

From these shafts, the king's life energy was propelled outside of the "life energy band" that surrounds our earth. His life energy continued at a specific trajectory while in the "time void," using space as a conductor and propulsion medium to transcend his energy onto the new world. This destination included a life form capable of supporting a human soul (right brain). The king's life energy would be the first to comingle (modify chromosome configuration) with the most "advanced" life form of the new planet. Many Egyptians then systematically followed as each day presented a new opportunity to join the king in the new world. Through evolution, many rudimentary animal characteristics were bred out effectively restarting the human race.

Once the alignment of the "first objective planet" was extinguished (out of alignment), a removable plug was used to block the adjacent tube to utilize a new location. These opposite destinations were used to ensure success of the Egyptians' objectives.

Subterranean chambers in the pyramid served as an event observation location that was used to fine tune event pressure via the "expansion chamber" (grand gallery), which was used to help control distance. This was achieved by moving a large granite slider wall from one end of the chamber to the other.

RELEASE MODULE

Located inside the king's chamber was a "resistor" container used to subdue the life energy for an instant before being directed through the propulsion channel. (The condition of the container suggests extreme usage.)

Once the dispatch event concluded, the deceased king was mummified and buried a distance away from the pyramids. This action was performed to leverage two objectives. The first was to separate his body from the dispatch area to avoid future life energy deflections. The second was to

Chapter 8 - The Ancient Egyptians

encompass his remains with items of love and devotion. This love demonstrated through the giving of material items augmented the connection between the gift providers and the king's life energy. Post-event mourning was designed to achieve intense levels, further assisting in the connection to the King. This "connection" accommodated the sequential life energies that followed.

The order in which individuals were dispatched carried merit; incorrect prioritization would jeopardize the strength of the connection. These trailing life energies followed the same path as the king while bombarding their new planet and assuming positions in similar life energy species. These events created many variations of the same human life energy version (different races).

To prevent the infection of impure life energies that might follow, select Egyptians volunteered to remain held to this earth and construct a facade that obstructed the entrance to the pyramid. At the same time, they removed the directional shaft occlusion to further distract would-be followers. These remaining Egyptians would be reborn as instructional advisories such as Einstein, Tesla, and Newton while restricted to this earth.

Shortly after this time period, the earth was subject to a series of meteor strikes, which caused an alteration of the earth's eco-system. This condition elevated the earth's water level for a period of time and washed away evidence of the Golden Age Egyptians with the exception of the four great pyramids and a sphinx.

SPHINX BURIED AT GIZA

Survivors of this catastrophe continued the Egyptian heritage by passing their knowledge from generation to generation. This information was used to restart traditional ancient Egypt.

GREAT SPHINX OF GIZA

Chapter 8 - The Ancient Egyptians

The sphinx of Giza illustrates a depiction of the king's elevated right-brain capabilities. Absent of political influence, this admiration for these right-brain advancements was exemplified as an aspiration. This monument faced the sunrise in the constellation of Leo in 10,500 BC.

Why They Did It

The Egyptian calendar encrypts rhythmic patterns that predicted the human existence timeline as a starting point, apex, and conclusion. King Osiris and his society existed at the pinnacle of the timeline. For the human race to survive beyond this world, an existence must be initiated on new life-sustaining planets.

Human life energy must vacate this planet as it recycles itself and continues into antiquity and eventually oblivion. The apogee of each human existence ensures our species survival by pollinating human life across the cosmos.

What They Left Behind

Following the Egyptian societal collapse, food shortages and political disputes produced widespread chaos. People then adopted cultural motifs that where formerly restricted. Regional uncertainty forced large groups of people to vacate the area and initiate various settlements. For the foreseeable future, these people endured hardships that can only be described as horrifying.

Eventually, local leaders gained control of their own resources and attempted to maintain a primary level of order. A monetary compensation system was enforced, which tracked individuals' work production and rewarded them accordingly.

While the area was returning to a somewhat normal state, the Greeks overpowered the region. While evaluating their new domain, they devised their own celestial solution, which included many human based gods such as Zeus and Apollo. These insufficient substitutes for improved personal energy produced jealousy, which resulted in the disfigurement of many Egyptian portraits.

Chapter 8 - The Ancient Egyptians

THE FALLEN

Community leaders were compelled to fabricate stories that would pacify and facilitate societal growth. These stories glorified exaggerated facts that would eventually become modern religions. The concept of heaven and hell is referred to as life energy advancement or digression throughout each lifetime. The concept of praying is transposed from the Egyptians holding the hands adjacent to their face and facing skyward, which enabled angelic comprehension.

COMMUNICATION TO OTHERS

Airborne images in the Peruvian Desert were created to exemplify the life energy forms contained on this planet. These "earth carvings" represented worldly attributes illustrating significant energy form such as fire, foliage, animals, insects, birds, and fish. These pictorials also communicated a successful human colonization of the planet.

NAZCA MONKEY

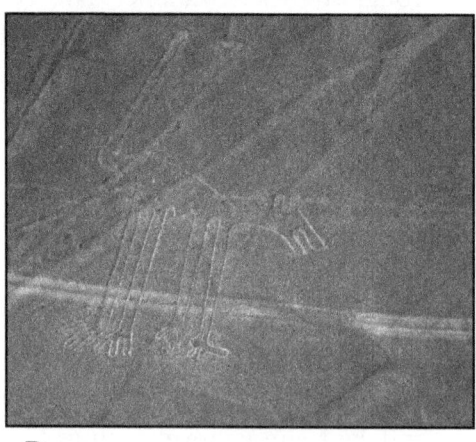

DOG

Chapter 8 - The Ancient Egyptians

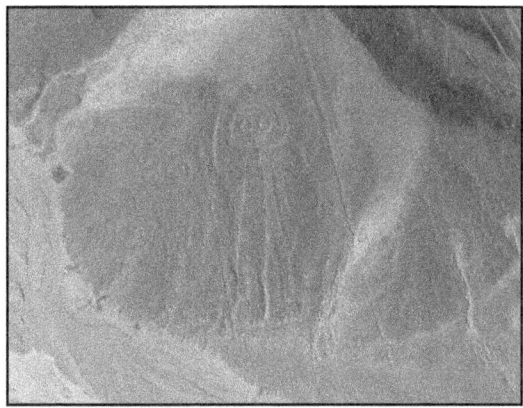

Nasca Astronaut

A mountain range in the Atacama Desert illustrates a sign of a large person informing additional travelers of a successful "human life energy" evolution.

Ancient Runway

A Nasca trapezoid in Peru features a runway constructed with small rocks designed to attract life energies to this planet.

TUH

Hieroglyphics carved into many of the structures and artifacts describe a lifestyle and objective the Egyptians accomplished on earth. These illustrations describe rituals meant to transcend throughout many generations with specific instructions that could be visible only to "like minded" people.

Due to the complexity of the Egyptian calendar, it was necessary for later societies to establish a new yearly calendar. This calendar would be created by using the most obvious celestial events.

With the Egyptian calendar ending in December of 2012 it shows not the ending of life on earth, instead, a new chapter of understanding to the explanation of our human existence.

Chapter 9
RELIGION

It would be impossible to spotlight a single event that has produced more human suffering on this planet than the discrepancies created by religion. Due to the many variations of religion, opinionated controversy was inevitable. Can one or all religions be correct? If there is a single supreme answer, who decides? The single most fact that drives religion is the fear of the unknown, which includes post life experiences. Though religion has created widespread torment throughout modern history, it's not all bad. Religion has contributed many positive attributes to our current human existence.

Events out of a person's control such as a death of loved one give humans an instinctual need to believe in something beyond their comprehension.

What was the world like before religion? This can be a difficult concept because most of us have been raised with one or more religions throughout our lifetime.

Why Our World

Post-Egyptian Period

Once ancient Egypt fell, the people remaining were subjected to widespread confusion while being exposed to remaining symbolism and other remnant information. Not knowing what to believe, they represented the proverbial blank slate. Many people disbursed and settled into various areas, where random events coupled with imagination would manifest stories created for the conscious well-being of the population.

This mental well-being was needed to comfort people in dire situations as well as attempting to curtail negative behavior. The "birth" of religion was produced by the simplification of ancient Egyptian events while adding fabrications from localized occurrences. These concepts incorporated existing attributes such as the human "spirit" traveling into the universe after death, while an underdeveloped soul is left behind and tortured.

Though many religious tails were fabricated, stories containing miracles with gore and violence gained a foothold. Once a particular story gained momentum, it embedded itself in the minds of the believers.

These theatrical presentations would transcend generations, becoming our modern-day scripture. A common component of many religions is the reference to heaven which is described as an incomprehensible experience. Particular religious days or holidays were highlighted and designated as a celebrated event further embedding the story.

The ancient Egyptians honored "energies" such as life, electricity, fire, and universe. This respect initiated religion's original "idea" of a "god" that included a human form to encourage solidification of the story.

Differences in this creative process included unique attributes resulting in "confusion," which made relating common religious attributes difficult. This disorientation produced disagreements that escalated into widespread aggravation.

Administration

Some religions suggest humans should always live in repentance. This observance to adversity is typical of negative minded people. The idea of happiness is a common human emotion that affects every person on the planet. The failure to achieve this common goal can be contributed to a lack of education.

Many religions fail to translate basic information that is mandatory for a positive life experience. Some establishments create mandatory regiments for their patrons designed to produce suffering and also humiliation which is used to entrench commitment.

Comparatively, experiencing this humiliation is more easily obtainable than self improvement. This easier path leads to low self-image which creates negative energy that eventually infects a person's life, producing both physical and mental illnesses.

Many people attend Sunday services at their local churches. When the sermon concludes, people engage socially before departing to their respective homes with little change made to their personal life energy. By nature, the only avenue to achieve personal energy advancement is through assisting the less fortunate. When this scenario is carried out personally, the results are exponential and produce appreciation for one's own life.

Religious establishments create ceremonies to bless the union between two people in marriage. Unfortunately, due to the absence of proper training, grim results wait for more than half of these participants. While many who remain in marriage do so unhappily to avoid the negative effects of divorce. Only a small percentage would be willing to repeat the process with the same partner. Luckily, there are no "standards of success" for these establishments.

Each society processes the death of a loved one uniquely. Religious establishments play a role in this process by producing a ceremony and gathering place for friends and loved ones to mourn the passing. With kind words from a pastor and loved ones, the deceased is remembered with dignity.

These funerals can vary from a traditional standpoint to the most bizarre, every ritual different from the next. Modern society's inconsistent response to such a substantial part of life leads one to believe nobody is sure what to do with the departed.

An institutionalized attitude among religious administrators has created a "business as usual" behaviorism. This complacent action has produced a "lag" that causes disinterest in future and current religious members. Redirection of these establishments will include an updateable interactive learning program that encapsulates "new era" ideas. In mature "enlightenment gatherings," subject matter will include a dialogue on how to create "heaven on earth." This happiness will be facilitated by intelligent choices throughout the courtship process. Such gatherings preparing people for life with "new age" training methods that build self-esteem, while making more successful love relationship choices and initiating positive family support systems.

Heaven and Hell

A common attribute built into religion is the promise of a post-death destination labeled as either "heaven" or "hell". An ambiguous tipping point that delivers an equal result regardless of the degree of acceptance to these opposing destinations.

These alternatives facilitate leverage over parishioners, enabling behavioral influence. This simple methodology helps control monetary donations to the satisfaction of the church administration while assuring contributors a safe passage into heaven.

Our world delivers daily experiences that contribute to a person's life energy. Actions and perception within these events produce variations of happiness. Energies associated with each thought or action produce a degree of negative or positive energy. Experiencing an extremely negative situation is viewed by the participant as being "hell" or a "hellish" event. Heavenly situations occur when recognition of positive energy consumes a person.

Acknowledgment of personal energy initiates the beginning of self-improvement. This is followed by a continuous oscillation between positive and negative perceptions. Positive lifestyles deplete negative energy while producing a "positive energy field" that moves life energy forward.

"Good energy" or heaven is maintained by a constant appreciation for each element contained within a lifestyle. When this appreciation falters, the "feeling" of heaven declines into a dormant state.

Chapter 9 - Religion

Material items provide temporary ingredients that cause heavenly feelings. Obtaining these items is more convenient than nurturing appreciation, a key ingredient for happiness.

While remaining neutral, millions of atheists do not accept a heaven and hell post death location concept.

God

As a society, we use the term and idea of "God" on a daily basis. A popular image of God is one of someone, somewhere pulling the strings to allow havoc or grant fortune for an unknown reason. Popular phrases for God include "God knows best" and "it's in God's hands now." These phrases are designed to promote confidence when the results of a situation conclude in a desirable fashion.

Some religions guarantee the appearance of a God upon death. This concept draws skepticism due to the absence of divine proof or the location in which this interaction could occur. Therefore, the idea of a "God" as a single entity is flawed. The phrase "God" is defined as "all-knowing," which is the exact opposite of our understanding of God.

Life's most difficult questions can be answered by the energy of "God." Energy "spiking" is produced when tragic events occur. As negative energy attempts to equalize, it produces positive human interactions. This "normal" process yields both painful and positive results.

Some call it karma; others refer to it as fate. Things happen that way they do because "life energy" forces the issue.

God is:

- Positive energy, all that is good in the world
- The universe and the energies contained within it
- The medium upon which all existence is constructed
- The energy responsible for each occurrence in a person's life
- The sensible voice inside people's conscious that guides a positive decision while ultimately controlling their life path
- The miracle of life and death

Choosing the correct life path is difficult due to a self-growth requirement which is uncomfortable. Once this hurdle has been overcome, exponential positive energy is obtained. Combining these steps constructs various levels of happiness.

Chapter 9 - Religion

Angels

Most religions include a version of an "angel" figure. This mythical assistant is credited with comforting people in desperate situations. Created from a variation of God, an angel is known for exhibiting similar unearthly powers capable of performing miracles for a beneficiary.

An angel is:

- A single parent with three kids holding everything together when love has failed
- A mother who puts everything aside to help her daughter who is hurting from a break up
- Someone who fixes a broken-down car for a family in distress and then disappears before gratitude is given
- Making room for an orphan while offering the family's love to the child.

Angels are people who have taken the idea of self-improvement and made it into a lifestyle, accommodating others while enhancing their own life energy.

TUH

All new establishments should be created for the well-being of people, a means to take care of each other, positive energy at full power. Discarded retail and administration buildings should be used to shelter the homeless and provide training while arranging placement of the unemployed back into the workforce.

Due to poor humanity training people are living a dissolute life while failing to recognize their purpose. Intelligence progresses as new information is discovered while updating previous beliefs. The idea of religion was conceptualized within a brief earthly time span and has produced centuries of turmoil. Each religion exhibits characteristics unique onto itself; almost none of these attributes can be proven.

Everyone needs something to believe in. Some people believe in nothing because they can't make sense of current religions. If a single religion were completely comprehensible it would stand out to everyone.

Proof of the ultimate religion has yet to be identified; logic dictates that, none of them are correct.

No matter the duration or intensity of any situation people are "living it" because they earned their lifestyle in a past or present life. The concept of heaven is the personal opinion of the individual. People can obtain the feeling of heaven by acknowledging the positive aspects present in their current surroundings. A divine destination is achieved in a single lifetime: happiness.

Chapter 10
VERSIONS OF YOU

The process of pacifying the conscious mind while allowing the unconscious mind to work sparks an idea into the conscious mind, which is then faced with the decision whether to accept the notion, or reject it. One can acknowledge positive and negative energy while collaborating with individuals to look for answers that may or may not exist. Once the acceptance of a new hypothesis transpires, advancement in the understanding of our human existence begins. No single person can be credited for the notations within these pages; the fact is that everyone in the world has played a part. The following chapter may push the envelope a little.

In every child-producing family there is a limited number of life energy placements open for fulfillment. These life vessels commonly support similar life energies that are subject to family energy levels.

There are noticeable physical and mental similarities when comparing particular family relatives. Familiar energies provide comfort to each other by exhibiting common physical and mental attributes, which, in turn, enhance the energy of the family unit. Family members are encouraged to adapt to conditions within the unit to preserve the structure. This natural compliance produces a common bond throughout life's triumphs and tragedies.

The path of each family is uniquely produced by the sum of their actions, which advance or decline family energy. These conditions alter life paths of family members, which are amplified after multiple lifetimes that advance or decline with each generation.

For family energy to endure the bloodline must continue. If family energy is allowed to discontinue (no offspring) the remaining life energies at the time of death become rogue and are then subject to "random selection," resulting in relocation into an accommodating family structure.

The Fabric

A person is removed from the time continuum when their body stops functioning. This person (right brain only) is instantly re-inserted back into the fabric as a newborn child. This entrance can transpire either forward or backward in the time fabric. Because life energies use many life spans to advance, new positions are filled using

Chapter 10 - Versions of You

mature and immature versions of the same life energy. In other words, when an infant is born, the life energy could still exist in an additional life instance such as a sibling, parent, or grandparent. These energy layers vary to accommodate and educate future and past life energy instances. This repetitive platform steadily advances individual life energy. Large families advance more rapidly due to the additional placements available. Instances of life energies then multiply exponentially.

Family evolution produces variations in "common" life energies, which occur naturally throughout many lifetimes. Identification of these equal life energies can be confirmed by comparing physical and mental characteristics such as personality, talent, habits, eye configuration, hair patterns, birth marks, body type, likes and dislikes.

It is not unusual for a family to produce a "breakout" life version (person). This condition is due to an abnormal energy progression from a previous life in a positive or negative direction. This energy spike is the result of extreme life-altering conditions that occur over a lifetime.

Our worldwide life energy advancement system will continue to function until global humanity is realized, which will then conclude the earth's purpose for humans.

TUH

The main structure of the earth will last for billions of years as each climate cycle ushers in the next phase of life forms. Every life-sustaining planet in the universe serves as a possible human energy advancement platform. By observing the evolution of our existence the Golden Age Egyptians realized perfection while pollinating our "human energy" across the cosmos. The departure event produced a mathematical prediction to the beginning of the next positive energy cycle.

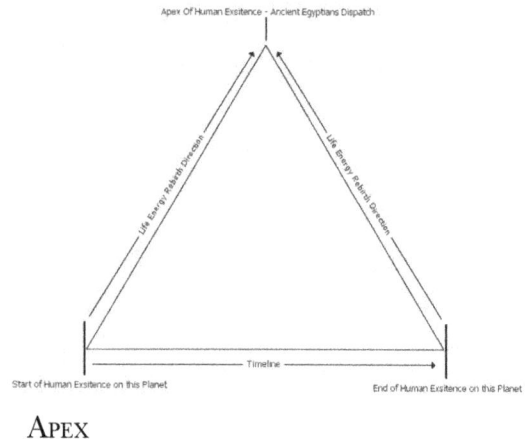

Apex

As present-day humans fully mature they are reborn back in time to the Golden Age Egyptian time period

Chapter 10 - Versions of You

where they are included in the departure to our next world.

Though clues exist to the Egyptians' destination, conclusive evidence is unclear regarding their final destinations.

The End

Version – 1.0

www.ingramcontent.com/pod-product-compliance
Lightning Source LLC
Chambersburg PA
CBHW051806040426
42446CB00007B/540